The Antholog

Blues
Guitar

The Anthology of

Blues Guitar

Transcriptions of 34 important blues songs and instrumentals forming a sampling of blues history from the Mississippi Delta to Chicago. Presented in standard music notation and tablature with vocal line and complete lyrics. Includes a special section on the music and techniques, brief biographies of the artists, and a discography.

by Woody Mann

Oak Publications
New York • London • Sydney

Edited by Peter Pickow

Order No. OK 64973
US International Standard Book Number: 0.8256.0315.3
UK International Standard Book Number: 0.7119.2870.3

Exclusive Distributors:
Music Sales Corporation
257 Park Avenue South, New York, NY 10010 USA
Music Sales Limited
8/9 Frith Street, London W1V 5TZ England
Music Sales Pty. Limited
120 Rothschild Street, Rosebery, Sydney, NSW 2018, Australia

Printed in the United States of America by
Vicks Lithograph and Printing Corporation

—To the memory of Rev. Gary Davis and Nick Perls

Table of Contents

Preface

Presented in this book is the music of twenty-seven artists whose recordings represent blues guitar playing at its best. It was enjoyable and challenging to use the entire spectrum of blues music as my pallet, without restricting myself to one style, artist, or technique. Easily the most difficult part in putting this project together was in selecting the contents. I wanted to include many of the major figures as well some of the more obscure players whose music is no less exciting and challenging. My aim was to cover as many bases as I could in terms of guitar styles and techniques in order to illustrate the rich tradition and the sounds of blues guitar playing.

These transcriptions are a loosely chronological collection of recordings of artists from the Delta to Chicago. The songs include tunes that were the blues 'hits' in their days—such as Robert Johnson's "Traveling Riverside Blues"— and well-known classics—like "Baby What You Want Me to Do," by Jimmy Reed. In addition, there are undiscovered (but no less brilliant) rarities like "South Carolina Rag," by Willie Walker, and Lonnie Johnson's "Away Down in the Alley Blues." Together, the songs offer a sampling of blues history. Some of the techniques covered in this collection include playing in five tunings and nine keys, bottleneck playing, syncopated picking styles, and a wide range of harmonic and melodic ideas. I chose one or two tunes from each player and in many cases could have easily transcribed a dozen. The choices by no means represent a summation of their work—only a sampler. Charlie Patton, Blind Blake, Big Bill Broonzy, Robert Johnson and Lonnie Johnson—to name a few—could easily have entire books devoted to their music. This project gave me a chance expand my own playing and a forum to include some of my favorite songs. I hope that these transcriptions will be useful to you in gaining some intimacy with the tunes so that you can spin further improvisations within this vital genre.

There are many ingredients that make up the music of a particular artist— most of which we may never know. It becomes an easy trap to broadly group the musicians and assign a certain technique or musical definition to a regional territory. These boundaries, mostly created by historians' speculations can be misleading. Like any musical tradition, the blues can sometimes be a bewildering and wonderfully confusing music that rarely conforms to a definition. The recordings themselves do not necessarily represent the complete picture of the music at the time. How many gifted musicians went unrecorded we will never know. In addition, it is difficult to view the music outside the environment in which it was played. Whatever was required for a playing situation—be it dances, the streets, the church, or the clubs—was probably the main factor in developing an individual style and sound.

The musicians spotlighted in this book lived all over the South from the rural areas to cities like Memphis, Jackson, St. Louis, and Chicago. In some areas there was one guitarist who was so influential and popular that many other players copied his style. These guitarists may have similar qualities in their playing but it does not necessarily outline a style. It is easy to hear the influence Charlie Patton had on his contemporaries in the Mississippi Delta or the impact Blind Blake had on the guitarists in the Carolinas. And, for example, certain specifics of guitar tunings and harmonic ideas are common to the playing of most guitarists from St, Louis. But when one listens to the music of Charlie Patton, Mississippi John Hurt, Bo Carter, and Robert Johnson—all from the Delta—it is easy to hear how completely different their playing was. The music of Texas musicians Blind Lemon Jefferson, Mance Lipscomb, Blind Willie Johnson, and Henry Thomas exhibit vastly differing approaches. Even in the playing of guitarists whose styles are more closely related, such as Rev. Gary Davis, Blind Boy Fuller, and Willie Walker (all from the Carolina area) one can easily discern significant differences. The nuances of sound and touch as well as the choice of harmonies—in short, all the things that make up the essence of the music—are unique to each player.

The influences of other musicians and their recordings serve to make the playing style of any single artist a composite of techniques, riffs, and repertoire from various sources. As an example, take the music of Robert Johnson, who was from Mississippi. The songs and guitar techniques of Scrapper Blackwell and Lonnie Johnson (both from St. Louis), Blind Blake (from Florida)—as well as the many sounds from the Delta—are all part of his own style. Big Bill Broonzy, Blind Willie McTell, Blind Lemon Jefferson, and Charlie Patton were able to capture a broad scope of repertoire, melodies, and guitar techniques (including different tunings and bottleneck work) from many sources. It would be difficult to describe one typical sound for any one of these artists.

Even though there sometimes appears to be a dominant song, guitar key, or melodic idea that was adopted in a certain region, categorizing blues music can miss the real mark. The main lesson is that the beauty of the music is in the individual artist: That's the only thing we know for sure. Each song has a story all its own but is also an extension of others. Whatever connections the players shared, their recordings demonstrate that—even though the initial audience is gone—originality is always at the center of the blues and that blues music is forever full of possibilities.

My thanks to Steven Calt for his writings, the notes on the artists, and his helpful insights about the music. After all this time our conversations are still full of discovery. Many thanks to Teresa Figueira and Nik Munson for their valuable help and support in putting this project together. And, of course, my love always to Florence Satinoff who, when I was too young to drive, would always find the time to take me to my lessons with Gary Davis—consistently giving support and encouraging my music. Lastly, although it is too late to thank him personally, my thanks to Nick Perls, for letting me devour his record collection.

Enjoy and good luck.

The Artists

Scrapper Blackwell

Francis (Scrapper) Blackwell crafted one of the most striking and elegant blues guitar sounds ever created. Of mixed black and Indian descent, he was born in South Carolina in 1903 and reared in Indianapolis, where he taught himself guitar in childhood. Most of his recordings were accompaniments behind the popular pianist Leroy Carr, whom he met in the late 1920s, and his efforts to persuade their producer to feature him as a soloist were largely unsuccessful. Although his recording career waned with Carr's death in 1935, he was still a superb guitarist when rediscovered in Indianapolis in 1959. His pugnacious personality had tragic consequences: he was shot to death in the wake of drunken argument in 1962.

Blackwell was one of the few blues guitarists who approached his instrument in terms of overall sound. "Kokomo Blues," recorded in 1928, has a clear separation of bass and treble lines. The contrast between the soft brush of the bass and the snapping treble line gives Blackwell's playing a distinctive, full sound. He creates additional fullness by using all six strings to sound chords. Whereas many guitarists who favored the key of D lowered the sixth string to D, Blackwell facilitated his bass sound by damping the low strings.

Blind Blake

Although renowned as one of the most skilled black guitarists of his generation, Blake remains a historically obscure, enigmatic figure. Virtually nothing is known of him beyond the fact that he hailed from Jacksonville, Florida, and was born Arthur Blake. He was apparently living in Chicago when he first recorded for Paramount Records in 1926. His debut record, "West Coast Blues," was the only commercially successful guitar instrumental of the era. His seventy-nine issued sides included blues, "rag" tunes, and instrumentals, some of which are unclassifiable. He faded into obscurity during the Depression and is said to have died in the early 1930s.

"Georgia Bound" and "Police Dog Blues" were both recorded at the same 1929 session and represented new motifs for Blake, whose recording career displayed almost continuous creativity. "Georgia Bound" uses Blake's distinctive bass rolls, double thumbing, and stoptime techniques, and is representative of his pieces in the key of C. Its melody is the same as that of Robert Johnson's "Four Until Late." The transcription covers the first two breaks as well as the introduction and first verse.

"Police Dog Blues," Blake's only accompaniment in open D, has a halftime feel created by bass "dropouts." The subtleties of the bass and treble interplay give the tune its lively bounce. The accompaniment uses some of the techniques of Blake's "Chump Man Blues." The transcription includes the guitar breaks as well as the introduction and first verse.

Big Bill Broonzy

One of the most famous figures in blues history, Broonzy was born William Lee Conley Broonzy in Mississippi in 1898 and was reared in Pine Bluff, Arkansas. He took up violin in childhood and is thought to have learned guitar in the 1920s after moving to Chicago. Although Broonzy began recording in 1927, he did not become commercially successful until the 1930s, when he emerged as one of the mainstays of Chicago's blues scene, usually recording as part of an ensemble unit. His appearance at a 1938 "Spirituals to Swing" concert in Carnegie Hall brought him to the attention of white audiences, and as his singles recording career declined in the late 1940s he discarded his electric guitar and assumed a new identity as a self-accompanied "folk" musician. By the time of his death in 1957 he had achieved considerable popularity in Europe, which he toured several times. Broonzy's fanciful *Big Bill Blues* (1955) was the first autobiography by a blues artist.

"Brownskin Shuffle" was recorded in 1927, and, although it is a duet (probably with Steel Smith), it is one of Broonzy's ragtime guitar masterpieces. It is in the key of C, and displays some similarities to Blind Blake's playing—but Broonzy's heavy attack gives the song the distinctive Broonzy stamp.

"Worrying You Off My Mind" showcases his guitar work in a song of unusual structure and melody in the key of E. Together with "Brownskin Shuffle," this tune gives a glimpse into the wide-ranging repertoire and playing styles that make up the music of this great musician.

Bo Carter

Bo Carter (the recording pseudonym of Bo Chatmon) was the most inventive bluesman of the 1930s. Born Armenter Chatmon in 1893, he originally worked with six musical brothers who formed a square-dance stringband in their native Bolton, a hill country town in central Mississippi. In this capacity he played tenor banjo and bass viol. His career as a solo guitarist dates to the early 1930s, when blindness caused him to work as a street musician. Between 1930 and 1940 he recorded 106 sides, nearly all of which feature only his own National guitar for accompaniment. For most of the decade he lived in the Delta town of Anguilla, Mississippi, performing for largely white audiences. Chatmon died in 1964.

"Who's Been Here" (1938) is an unusual version of a turn-of-the-century "rag" staple, "Alabama Bound." It uses open G-style chord positions but is played in the same DGDGBE tuning as "Away Down in the Alley Blues." The song uses two chords. I have notated a few of its more unusual positions. It has a fast $\frac{4}{4}$ feel, but the accenting sometimes shifts to $\frac{2}{4}$. For clarity's sake, the transcription stays in $\frac{2}{4}$. The introduction, first verse, and break are transcribed.

Reverend Gary Davis

Gary Davis was one of the few black guitarists of his generation who devoted himself to acquiring instrumental expertise. While his emphasis on instrumentation did not hold great allure for his original Southern audience, it brought him singular prestige in the 1960s, and attracted numerous guitar students. Born in 1896 in Larens, South Carolina, Davis took up banjo and guitar in childhood. After becoming completely blind he became a gospel singer, eventually situating himself in Durham, North Carolina, a city of over 50,000. He had been an ordained Baptist minister for two years when he first recorded as "Blind Gary" in 1935 for the American Record Company, cutting two blues and twelve gospel titles, including "I Am the Light of This World. He moved to New York in the early 1940s, settling on 169 Street in the South Bronx. He continued playing on Harlem streets until the early 1960s, when he was already an acclaimed figure on the burgeoning "folk" circuit. His "Sampson and Delilah" became a pop hit for Peter, Paul and Mary. Davis was still performing at the time of his death in 1972.

Davis had a unique ability to play melody, syncopate the rhythm with his bassline, and simultaneously move his chords in a voice leading nature. Rather than play a simple G to C progression he would use two, three, or four separate voices in this cadence, creating a very thick guitar sound. I always thought that Davis's distinctive style of voice leading was partly an outgrowth of his experience at leading church congregations.

"I Am the Light of This World" is one of my favorite Davis tunes and one of the first I learned from him. It was recorded in the 1960s and is played in the key of C, in which Davis performed both religious songs and "rag" pieces like "Hesitation Blues," "I Belong to the Band," and "Buck Dance." Transcribed are the first verse and chorus.

"Make Believe Stunt," a version of "Maple Leaf Rag" in the key of A, is transcribed from another sixties recording and was one of Davis's main guitar instrumentals. Although it is basically a set-piece, Davis was constantly offering different subtleties and nuances when he performed it, even while playing with a heavy, hard approach. Some of his variations are noted in the transcription, which features all four main parts of the piece.

Snooks Eaglin

A vastly underrated guitarist, Eaglin has spent his entire life in New Orleans, where he was born Fird Eaglin in 1936. He began playing at age six and worked both as a rhythm and blues accompanist and as a solo street singer in the early 1950s. In 1958, at the age of 22, he recorded an album for Folkways that established him as the most original, accomplished guitarist of his time. Partly because of his lack of long-standing credentials, he played no part in blues concerts of the following two decades. Today he works primarily as a rhythm and blues session guitarist, occasionally appearing at blues festivals.

"Come Back Baby," which Eaglin acquired from a Lightnin' Hopkins recording and recorded in 1958, has been a blues standard since it was first recorded by Walter Davis in 1940.

Blind Boy Fuller

One of the most popular blues recording artist of the 1930s, Fuller was born Fulton Allen in 1908 in Wadesboro, North Carolina. He began playing in the mid 1920s and became a professional street singer after losing his sight in the late 1920s. In the early 1930s he settled in Durham, North Carolina, there learning guitar pointers from Gary Davis, whom he met in 1935. Fuller made his recording debut the same year and immediately became a leading commercial attraction; over the next five years he churned out some 135 sides, including "Weeping Willow" (1937) and "Meat Shakin' Woman" (1938). He was still active on the recording scene when he died in Durham in 1941.

The beautifully intricate "Weeping Willow" uses many passing chords and constantly moving melodic motifs. It is a complete guitar piece in itself, with the introduction, verse, and break all featuring the same guitar part. The way the chords resolve in their voicings is very reminiscent of Gary Davis's playing.

"Meat Shakin' Woman" uses some of the same voice leading ideas as "Weeping Willow." Both are set accompaniments. Guitarwise, "Meat Shakin' Woman" is similar to "I Am the Light of This World" and "Georgia Bound." The guitar part of the first verse is the same as that of the intro, and the $\frac{2}{4}$ bar appears in every verse.

Son House

A backsliding Baptist minister who became a quintessential Delta bluesman, Eddie James ('Son') House was born in 1902 in Lyon, Mississippi, a small town near Clarksdale. Soon after he first began singing blues at a Lyon house party in 1926, he took guitar pointers from a local musician. In 1930 he landed in Lula, Mississippi, and met Charlie Patton, who arranged for him to record for Paramount that year. In the early 1930s he worked as a tractor driver in Lake Cormorant, moving to Rochester, New York, shortly after being recorded by the Library of Congress in 1942. He was rediscovered in 1964 and became a popular blues concert attraction. House died in 1988.

"County Farm Blues" is the Library of Congress recording of a piece House first recorded in 1930 in response to a solicited "tribute" to Blind Lemon Jefferson. It is based on the melody of the latter's famous "See That My Grave Is Kept Clean," with lyrics reflecting House's own tribulations as a Parchman Farm prisoner in the late 1920s. Although the song is structurally akin to "rag" tunes rather than blues, House's guitar technique gives it the aura of a blues. The accompaniment follows the melody and is based on a rhythmic bass riff.

Mississippi John Hurt

Hurt was born in 1894 and spent nearly his entire life in the Delta town of Avalon, Mississippi, which numbered fewer than one hundred persons in the 1920s. He taught himself guitar in 1903 and began performing at local parties some three or four years later. He afterwards worked as a sharecropper and played primarily for his own entertainment. In the 1920s his main performance outlet was the white square dance, which found him flatpicking behind the fiddle of a white neighbor, Willie Narmour, thus forming virtually the only racially integrated combo known to exist then in the South. His two OKeh sessions in 1928 resulted in twelve issued sides. In 1963 he was rediscovered in Avalon and immediately became one of the most popular "folk" attractions of the period. After living briefly in Washington, D.C., he returned to Avalon, where he died in 1966.

"Candy Man," a song of Hurt's own composition recorded in 1928, was his most popular piece among 1960s audiences. It has an unusual accompaniment. The set guitar arrangement uses Hurt's characteristic alternating bass pattern. Hurt's approach is similar to that found in open tuning bottleneck pieces like Fred McDowell's "You Got to Move" in that the guitarist concentrates on capturing the vocal melody. In so doing Hurt departs from the chord shapes to play melodic notes, causing the bass and the rest of the chord to have a "dead" sound. The E chord he uses is an awkward position.

"Ain't No Tellin'," a version of "Pallet on the Floor" performed in the key of C and recorded in 1928, similarly follows the vocal melody and uses an alternating bass, which has a soft brushing quality. The verses begin on the F chord.

Elmore James

Elmore James was the only important postwar blues artist who never appeared before white concert audiences. James, whom B.B. King once credited as being his earliest guitar influence, was born in 1918 and reared in the hills south of the Mississippi Delta. His career dates to the early 1930s, when it was centered around the Delta town of Belzoni. Although a versatile slide guitarist, his most noteworthy influence was Robert Johnson, whose boogie approach he would adapt to a smooth band format. He began recording in 1951, achieving far greater success than his mentor, who lacked his elasticity as a vocalist and accompanist. He died in 1963 in Chicago.

His debut recording "Dust My Broom" was based on "I Believe I'll Dust My Broom," the primary Johnson piece James incorporated into his repertoire. The version presented here was recorded in 1953 on Chess.

Skip James

Although James had only a small reputation among his peers of the 1920s, he is regarded as one of the greatest blues artists of all time. Born Nehemiah James in 1902, he was reared in Bentonia, a hill country town south of the Mississippi Delta. He learned guitar in childhood and first played professionally around 1918 when he worked as a pianist in Weona, Arkansas. Soon afterwards he acquired the open E minor tuning in which he cast most of his guitar pieces. His single session in 1931 (for Paramount Records) resulted in 18 issued sides and established him as the only bluesman of the period to excel on both guitar and piano. Late in 1931, James began studying for the ministry. He made only sporadic subsequent forays into secular music until his rediscovery in Tunica, Mississippi, in 1964 when he was resurrected as a blues artist. He died in 1969 while living in Philadelphia.

"Devil Got My Woman" was recorded in 1931 and was James's main performance piece. It was later adapted by Robert Johnson, who recorded it as "Hellhound on My Trail." It has a free flowing structure and a modal sound stemming from the way that James implies simultaneous D Major and D Minor chords. Unlike his other pieces in open E minor tuning, it is played in D rather than E.

Blind Lemon Jefferson

A peerless vocalist and unique musician, Jefferson stood second to Bessie Smith as the most commercially appealing blues artist of the 1920s, yet few concrete details are known of his career. He was reared in Wortham, Texas, a small town sixty miles south of Dallas, and he traveled widely as an itinerant street singer. His hugely successful recording debut in 1926 sparked the vogue for self-accompanied blues singers. In the late 1920s he spent time in both Dallas and Chicago, and he is said to have died in Chicago in late 1929.

"Shuckin' Sugar," in Spanish tuning (open G), is one of Jefferson's most beautiful songs and is an atypical blues in terms of its structure and melody. His accompaniment—typical of many of his tunes—is a constant improvisation around the vocal line. The transcription has almost a fragmented look because of the partial chords and riffs set to varying rhythms and constantly changing barlines. This is one to listen to carefully. The transcription covers the first verse.

Lonnie Johnson

One of the most polished guitarists of his generation, Alonzo (Lonnie) Johnson originated an unequaled style of single-string lead fingerpicking. Born in New Orleans in 1889 or 1894, he took up violin as a youth and began playing guitar around 1917. By the early 1920s he had settled in St. Louis. After playing violin in Charlie Creath's local jazz band, he organized a trio with a violin-playing brother and a pianist. His recording debut on OKeh in 1926 brought him popularity second only to that of Blind Lemon Jefferson's, and by 1932 he had recorded some 130 sides, more than any male blues singer of the time. His recording career was eventually short-circuited when he resisted efforts to diversify his familiar brand of playing. After interludes in Chicago, Cincinatti, and Philadelphia (where he was working as a hotel janitor when rediscovered in the early 1960s), he moved to Toronto, dying there in 1970.

"Away Down in the Alley Blues" (1928), one of the few blues guitar instrumentals of the era, is one of Johnson's masterpieces. It is a three-chord blues instrumental played in a single-string style that serves to outline each chord. Its uniqueness lies in the fact that Johnson plays it fingerstyle, adding a syncopated bass to produce a swinging beat. It employs a modified dropped D tuning (DGDGBE), with the fifth string lowered to G, that is tailor-made for pieces in D. Since there is no set accompaniment to his improvisations, and because it is so unique, I transcribed the entire recording.

Robert Johnson

The most storied figure in blues history, Johnson was born in 1912 and reared in the Delta town of Commerce, just below Memphis. Originally a harmonica player, he took up guitar in the late 1920s, learning from such musicians as Son House. Around 1932 he moved to Arkansas and worked largely as an itinerant street musician. Recording sessions in 1936 and 1937 resulted in twenty-nine sides, one of which ("Terraplane Blues") was a modest hit of the period. In 1938, he was fatally poisoned while playing near Greenwood, Mississippi, allegedly by a "house frolic" employer who had discovered Johnson's affair with his wife. Posthumously, Johnson became the most copied guitarist of his generation.

"Traveling Riverside Blues" was a version of "Roll and Tumble," a Mississippi bottleneck standard of pre–World War I vintage designed for the then-popular 'Shimmy-She-Wobble' and later resurrected by Muddy Waters. Its main riff is difficult to execute: Johnson drags off the sixth string at the fourth fret in a roll-like fashion that gives the riff a soft bounce and brushlike sound. Like Charlie Patton, Johnson plays the riff in assorted ways without changing its notes. The transcription has all of the tune's variations in fingering for the introduction and first four verses.

"I Believe I'll Dust My Broom" was Johnson's second recording, and thus undoubtedly one of his basic repertoire pieces. One of Johnson's most innovative and beautiful tunes, it displays his ability to wrest the most subtle sounds and sonorities from the guitar. It is interesting to note that Johnson used three tunings for songs with his bass boogie accompaniment: the dropped D of "Dust My Broom," standard E (for "When You Got a Good Friend" and "Sweet Home Chicago"), and open D (for "Rambling on My Mind").

Tommy Johnson

Johnson was born in 1894 and reared in Terry, Mississippi, a town below Jackson. He became a musician around 1914 after running away from home and spending two years in the Delta. During the 1920s Johnson was the most popular bluesman in Jackson; his signature songs were local standards. His three recording sessions between 1928 and 1930 resulted in twelve issued sides. Johnson was still performing at the time of his death in 1956.

Johnson learned "Bye Bye Blues," a version of Charlie Patton's famous "Pony Blues," from a Drew, Mississippi, guitarist named Dick Bankston around 1914 and recorded it as a guitar duet fourteen years later. Besides the intro and first verse, I have written out an alternate verse. To add fullness to the transcription, I have also incorporated some of the playing of Johnson's duet partner, Charlie McCoy.

Blind Willie Johnson

An unsurpassed slide guitarist and the greatest gospel performer of his generation, Blind Willie Johnson is thought to have been born in 1900 in Marlin, Texas, a town numbering 4,300 persons in 1920. In the late 1920s he moved to Dallas, where he was first recorded in 1927. Between 1927 and 1930 he recorded some thirty sides—half of them vocal duets with his wife. By 1928 he had settled in Beaumont, Texas, where he was still performing at the time of his death in the 1940s.

"God Moves on the Water" was recorded in 1929. It recounts the 1912 *Titanic* tragedy, which resulted in 1,500 deaths and became grist for fundamentalists because its owner was alleged to have claimed that not even God would be able to sink the ship. It has a one-chord tonality, with a bottleneck accompaniment that follows the melody of the vocal. The transcription covers the intro, verse, and break.

Leadbelly

Leadbelly was the first blues guitarist to become a concert performer, and he did so without modifying the approach he took as a Southern dance entertainer. Born Huddie Ledbetter in 1889, he was reared in Leigh, Texas, a town near Shreveport that numbered only 500 people in 1930. His local career dates to around 1906. Most of his tunes were played on the twelve-string guitar. While serving a term in Angola Prison in 1933, he was discovered by John Lomax of the Library of Congress and taken under the latter's wing. Leadbelly soon settled in Brooklyn, New York, and plied his profession over the next fifteen years in urban "folk" forums, displaying an astonishing number and assortment of tunes. He died in 1949. The following year, the Weavers created the year's best-seller with a rendition of his "Irene."

"C.C. Rider" was Leadbelly's novel 1935 treatment of an enduring blues standard that was widely known in Texas before the First World War and served as Ma Rainey's signature song. In 1957 it was revived as a rock and roll hit by Chuck Willis, eventually reaching Number 12 on the national charts. Leadbelly's accompaniment follows the melody, with the bottleneck often sounding full chords.

Mance Lipscomb

Lipscomb's belated discovery in 1960 preserved vintage dance music he had played decades before, during the original heyday of the blues. He was born in 1895 and began playing guitar around 1909. As an adult he worked as a sharecropper who played for weekend dances, primarily in his home town of Navasota, Texas, which numbered some 5,100 people in 1930. Following his discovery in Navasota he recorded numerous albums and appeared regularly on the concert circuit before dying in 1976. "Sugar Babe," recorded in 1960, was derived from a local guitarist named Sam Collins and was the first song Lipscomb ever learned. It uses an alternating bass, with the melody played on top near its basic chord positions.

Memphis Minnie

The most famous of all female blues guitarists, Memphis Minnie, was born Lizzie Douglas in 1897 and reared in Walls, a Delta town just below Memphis. She began playing around 1908 and soon became an itinerant street singer. From the 1920s onward she was situated in Memphis. She began her long recording career in 1929 and enjoyed a hit record the following year with "Bumble Bee." By the time World War II disrupted the recording industry, she had produced 154 sides—usually in tandem with a backing guitarist. Her postwar recording career ended in 1954. A stroke prevented her from resuming her career during the subsequent blues revival, and she died in 1973 in Memphis.

"Drunken Barrelhouse Blues," the only tune in this collection played in the key of G, is a twelve-bar blues using standard chord positions for that key. Minnie plays a steady bass to help create a driving beat. The guitar break is outstanding.

Fred McDowell

Like Mance Lipscomb, McDowell was a sharecropper who had never worked as a professional musician at the time of his belated discovery. A native of Tennessee, born in 1904, he spent most of his life in Mississippi. Around 1940 he settled in the Delta town of Como, where he was discovered in 1959. Although McDowell played electric guitar, he used an acoustic picking approach; nearly all of his works featured bottleneck presentation. He died in 1972.

"You Got to Move," a close melodic relative of "Sittin' on Top of the World," was recorded in 1965 and afterwards popularized as a rock song by the Rolling Stones. McDowell's accompaniment is a complete guitar work in itself. The guitar part follows the vocal melody around a D tonality.

Blind Willie McTell

A street singer who usually played a twelve-string guitar, McTell was born in 1901 in Thomson, Georgia. He began playing guitar around 1914, learning from his mother. Without having an appreciable "hit" record, he nevertheless managed to record some forty-six singles for various commercial companies between 1927 and 1935. In 1940 he was extensively recorded by the Library of Congress.

He was still an effective guitarist when he recorded nine years later for the newly formed Atlantic Records. He became a preacher shortly before his death in 1959.

"Statesboro Blues," a tune McTell recorded at his second session in 1928, refers to the Georgia town (population 4,000 in 1930) northwest of Savannah in which he was reared. It has a loosely textured accompaniment with a fairly steady bass. McTell's hybrid pick uses so many techniques that no single one is representative of his sound. It has an unusual $\frac{2}{4}$ bar for the pickup to the G chord. Instead of playing the usual full V chord McTell only hints at it. The transcription contains the introduction, first verse, and bridge.

Charlie Patton

A truly inspired guitarist and performer, Charlie Patton was Mississippi's first blues celebrity. Born in 1891, he was reared on the Delta plantation of Dockery and took up guitar around 1907. By the time he first recorded for Paramount in 1929, he was long established as the state's leading blues dance entertainer. The commercial success of his "Pony Blues" and "High Water Everywhere" led him to record more sides in a single year (forty-one) than any bluesman of the period. He died in 1934, three months after his final record session.

"Screamin' and Hollerin' the Blues" (1929), one of Patton's first guitar efforts and basic blues themes, was designed for the 'Shimmy-She-Wobble'. Its complicated picking is sometimes reminiscent of banjo playing, replete with frailing, strumming, and pick rolls. I wrote out variations of the descending bass riff because Patton constantly changes its accenting and shifts the downbeat. The vocal and guitar part contain different accenting, giving the effect of two simultaneous downbeats. The first verse is written exactly as Patton played it, with an alternate verse included, along with two variations of the first four bars of the song.

"Green River Blues" (1929) was Patton's esoteric adaptation of the first tune he learned. Its title lyric refers to a small creek and lumber-camp settlement near the Delta town of Lake Cormorant, Mississippi. The accompaniment demonstrates how sound is at the very center of Patton's playing. The main E-chord riff has simultaneous bass and treble lines, and the texture and depth of sound Patton obtains by playing a simple E chord is difficult to recreate. Patton also explores different sonorities by playing the same notes in a chord two or three different ways. Its $\frac{2}{4}$ bar is part of the song's basic structure.

Jimmy Reed

Originally a church singer like John Lee Hooker, Reed was born in 1925 in the Mississippi Delta town of Dunleith. He did not play professionally until the late 1940s when he was situated in Chicago. Following his commercial debut in 1953, he had a successful, decade-long career as a rhythm and blues recording artist on VJ Records, amassing ten national rhythm and blues hits that established him as the last great blues songwriter. "Bright Lights Big City" (1961), his final commercial success, became the title of a best-selling 1984 novel. He died in 1976.

"Baby What You Want Me to Do" is a vocal duet between Reed and his wife; I have included her vocal harmony part in the transcription.

Henry Townsend

Henry Townsend remains the only living blues performer with roots in the 1920s. Born in 1909 and reared in Cairo, Illinois, he has lived in St. Louis since the late 1920s. Although exposure to Lonnie Johnson first inspired him to excel on guitar, his most direct influence was Henry Spaulding, the local musician who popularized "Cairo Blues." Improbably, he attained striking inventiveness within a one-chord, loosely structured blues framework that was usually the province of pedestrian players. Townsend was still something of a novice when he first recorded such works as "Mistreated Blues" for Columbia in 1929; he enjoyed four scattered recording sessions between 1929 and 1937, amounting to twelve sides. Henry is currently living in St. Louis and still playing up a storm.

"Mistreated Blues" was one of the most difficult tunes in this collection to transcribe. It is played around an E chord, with Townsend using open E minor tuning to create unusual sounds and dissonances. His intricate picking style employs brushing, snapping strings, and bending, all done over a driving bass. Because it has no accenting other than the driving beat, it can be thought of as played with a $\frac{1}{1}$ feel.

Willie Walker

A little-known but locally dominant blues figure who was extolled by Josh White as a guitar equivalent of Art Tatum, Walker was born in 1896 in South Carolina. By 1910 he was living in Greenville, South Carolina, and working in a stringband that included Gary Davis. The two surviving sides Walker recorded at his single 1930 session in tandem with backing guitarist Sam Brooks are unusual for a blind musician in that they feature a dance beat. Having recorded a fraction of his repertoire, Walker died in 1933.

"South Carolina Rag (Take 2)" has very intricate picking and is among the fastest, cleanest, and most inventive guitar pieces of its era. I have transcribed all of its guitar variations and riffs.

Muddy Waters

The most commercially successful postwar bluesman, Muddy Waters was born McKinley Morganfield in 1915 and reared in Clarksdale, Mississippi. Originally a harmonica player like Robert Johnson, he took up guitar around 1932, featuring bottleneck presentation absorbed from such artists as Johnson and Son House. He was a locally based, part-time player when recorded by the Library of Congress in 1941. In 1943 Waters moved to Chicago and began heading loose-knit combos that included piano, drums, harmonica, and his newly purchased electric guitar. After his recording debut in 1948, he produced such hits as "Rollin' Stone" (1950), "Louisiana Blues" (1951), and "Hoochie Coochie Man" (1954). Once his singles career waned in the mid 1950s he became a concert attraction for white audiences. Waters died in 1983.

"I Be's Troubled," a Library of Congress recording, was the acoustic predecessor of his first commercial hit, "I Can't Be Satisfied," recorded in 1948. It is an unusually phrased bottleneck blues based on a single tricky riff, with the sixth bar delivered in $\frac{2}{4}$ time.

Howlin' Wolf

Howlin' Wolf was already a veteran blues singer when he appeared as a Chess Records commodity in 1951. Born Chester Burnett in 1910, he learned guitar while living in Ruleville, Mississippi, in the late 1920s; one of his early tutors was Charlie Patton. In the early 1930s he became a popular harmonica player in the Mississippi and Arkansas Delta. Wolf began working as a disk jockey in West Memphis, Arkansas, in 1948 and was discovered three years later by Ike Turner. His recording success led him to relocate to Chicago. Using a small combo, Wolf garnished R&B hits in 1956 with "Smokestack Lightnin'" and "I Asked for Water," based on a decades-old Tommy Johnson theme. He died in 1976.

"Ain't Goin' Down That Dirt Road" was one of Wolf's rare acoustic guitar offerings, ventured in a London studio during a 1968 session. It has a drone sound and features a single-riff accompaniment based on an E chord.

The Transcriptions

My intention was to transcribe as exact a replica of the recordings as possible without using many confusing and misleading complexities. In this way, the transcriptions may be used to help clarify the music and can also become a tool for learning directly from the recordings. For each song I wrote out the introduction, first verse, and at least one of the guitar breaks. In a few, I included other verses or parts of verses to illustrate variations on phrases that may be played more than one way. Since most of the musicians are improvising in some way, the opening verse may not illustrate the basic picking, chord forms, syncopation, or riffs. In these tunes, rather than write out the entire piece, I included an alternate verse. This is sort of a composite of these elements written out in a less confusing way. For example, in many of the songs the meter is continually shifting—sometimes as part of the structure (as in Bo Carter's "Who's Been Here"), other times at the whim of the player (as in "Shuckin' Sugar" by Blind Lemon Jefferson). The same is true of the way the bar structures change from verse to verse. Instead of making a judgement call, or changing the guitar part, I wrote out the first verse as played and organized the tune more clearly in the alternate verse. My intention was to not to get excessively technical with a music that sometimes can (and most times should) elude analysis—it was just to be accurate.

The basic meter of most of the songs is $\frac{4}{4}$ (with many implied meters), but for clarity a few songs are written in $\frac{12}{8}$. In addition, all of the tunes are written out in the guitar key—rather than the absolute key. For example, if a song is played in the key of C with a capo on the second fret (raising it to the key of D), I transcribed it in C. The same is true for the open tunings: If the song is played in open G tuning with the guitar tuned a whole step low, I transcribed it in G not F.

Legend of Music Symbols

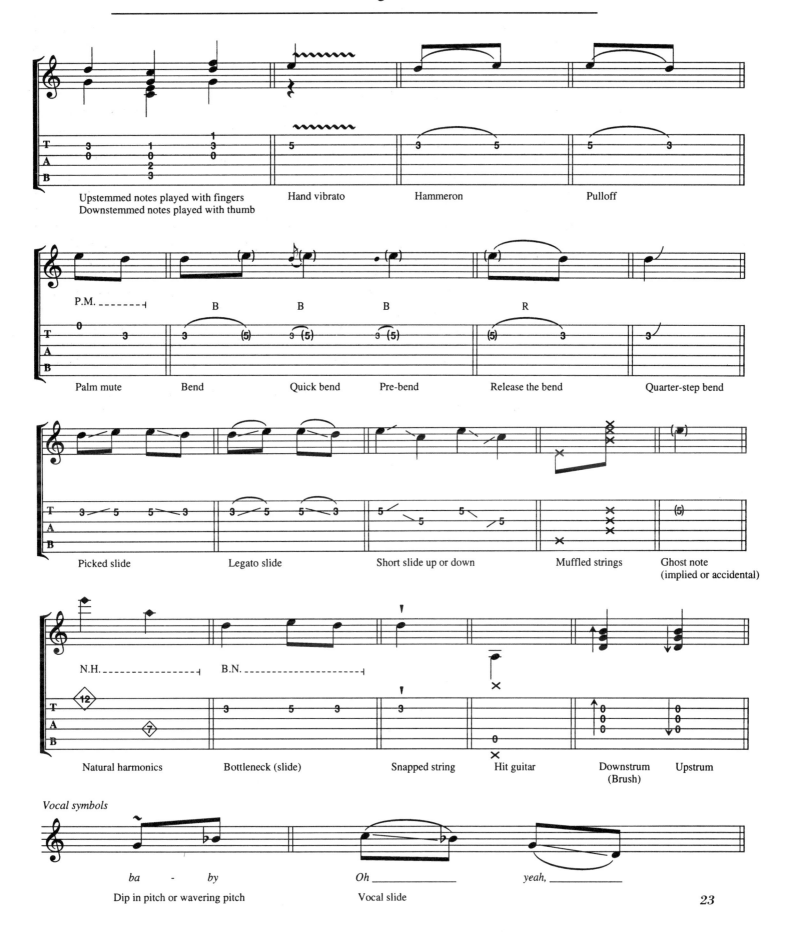

Upstemmed notes played with fingers
Downstemmed notes played with thumb

Hand vibrato

Hammeron

Pulloff

Palm mute

Bend

Quick bend

Pre-bend

Release the bend

Quarter-step bend

Picked slide

Legato slide

Short slide up or down

Muffled strings

Ghost note
(implied or accidental)

Natural harmonics

Bottleneck (slide)

Snapped string

Hit guitar

Downstrum
(Brush)

Upstrum

Vocal symbols

ba - by

Dip in pitch or wavering pitch

Oh _____

Vocal slide

yeah, _____

A Note on the Music and Technique

You know . . . you have the quarter notes and half notes . . . you figure that out, you understand. But then you have to give it a beat—some kind of rhythm—because, you know, that's the whole thing. . . . Now a melody, yeah— that can be trouble.

—Rev. Gary Davis

There are so many playing techniques and styles used throughout these songs that it can be tricky to see the relationships among them. Even though the chords, riffs, and melodies are unique to each tune there is a common idea in the picking approach that enables you to see a connection. This *fingerstyle* picking is basically a two-line idea—the bass line is played with the thumb, and the treble line is played with the fingers. That is why the music is notated with double stems (up-stems for treble, down-stems for bass). One of the goals in developing a well-grounded picking technique is to achieve independence of rhythm and sound between these two lines. The greater the degree of independence, the easier it becomes to negotiate the syncopation and capture the nuances of the music. It also provides a more natural backdrop over which to add many other idiomatic blues guitar techniques, such as damping, bending, brushing, and snapping. It is this basic contrapuntal picking idea—rather than an organized pattern-pick approach—that is at the foundation of all fingerpicking guitar styles. The music of the thirty guitarists in this collection illustrates this picking approach in thirty different ways.

The following excerpts demonstrate a few contrasting approaches to common instrumental phrases and styles and provide illustrations of some of the various ways that the treble and bass parts can play off one another. The first example is a phrase from the playing of Blind Blake, one of the greatest of the ragtime blues guitarists. The bass, in addition to being on the beat is dragged across one, two, or three strings as the pickup to the next beat. These *thumb rolls* have no constant pattern to them—they are just a natural part of Blake's playing.

The second excerpt is a phrase from Robert Johnson's "Traveling Riverside Blues." His sound is completely different from Blind Blake's, but the picking idea and technique in this example are the same: the bassline provides the pickup to the next beat. The main riff, played different ways, is characterized by the syncopation of the bass thumb rolls.

Tuning: D G D G B D

The following example is typical of the playing of Mississippi John Hurt. His sound is typified by a steady alternating bass on the beat with a syncopated melody on top.

The playing of Lonnie Johnson is excerpted in this next example. The long melodic lines seem to bounce off the bass, punctuating the phrase. There is no pattern picking at all in his playing—only the facility to articulate his improvisations with incredible speed, alacrity, and feeling.

Tuning: D G D G B E

In the last example you'll find another Blind Blake passage. This one is from "Police Dog Blues," played in Open D tuning. The halftime feel is due to the way the bass line drops out—creating the stoptime syncopation.

Tuning: D A D F# A D

It often confuses the issue to get too technical in analyzing this music. Developing a good foundation is the best way to avoid a lot of needless analysis. It is a good idea to play the songs slowly with just the bassline to get the feel, then add the treble line. Start with songs that are less syncopated and in which the bass notes fall on the beat (as in "Ain't No Tellin' " by Mississippi John Hurt or Mance Lipscomb's "Sugar Babe"). Once you have a good feel for this relatively simple style, you'll find it much easier to master the tunes in which the picking is less organizedthose of Blind Lemon Jefferson, Scrapper Blackwell, or Charlie Patton, for instance.

When I was taking lessons with Rev. Gary Davis, I remember trying to work out a tune as a set composition—right down to the last note. When I would go back to my next lesson he would always play the tune with a different twist or improvise entire new phrases within the song. This drove me crazy until I realized that he was teaching me his style and approach to playing—not just a collection of songs. Playing his fantastic guitar pieces became a logical kickoff point for me in learning the music of other blues and ragtime players whose music did not resemble his at all. This is something to keep in mind when exploring the wonderful variety of sounds that the great blues and ragtime guitarists have to offer.

Here is a breakdown of the keys and tunings.

Key	Tuning	Song
C	Standard	Georgia Bound Meat Shakin' Woman I Am the Light of This World Ain't No Tellin' Brownskin Shuffle South Carolina Rag
E	Standard	Green River Blues Sugar Babe Worrying You off My Mind Baby What You Want Me to Do Bye Bye Blues Ain't Goin Down That Dirt Road
A	Standard	Come Back Baby Weeping Willow Candy Man
G	Standard	Drunken Barrel House Blues
D	Standard	Kokomo Blues
D	Drop D	Statesboro Blues I Believe I'll Dust My Broom (Johnson)
D	Drop D and G	Away Down in the Alley Blues
G	Drop D and G	Who's Been Here
E minor	Open E Minor	Mistreated Blues
D minor	Open D minor	Devil Got My Woman
D	Open D	Police Dog Blues Dust My Broom (James) God Moves on the Water You Got to Move
G	Open G	County Farm Blues I Be's Troubled Shuckin' Sugar Traveling Riverside Blues Screamin' and Hollerin' the Blues C.C. Rider

The Tunes

You play just what you know . . . that's all you can do. Then, you understand, its all quiet when you go up against anybody . . . just play what you know. You go out in the world and say what you got to say . . . that's all.

—Rev. Gary Davis

Shuckin' Sugar

recorded by Blind Lemon Jefferson

Tuning: D G D G B D
Moderately

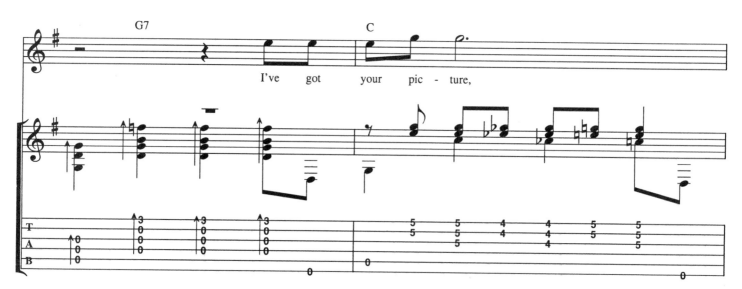

I put it in _____ a frame, _____ shuck - in' sug - ar, _____

And then if you _____ leave town, _ we can _ spot _

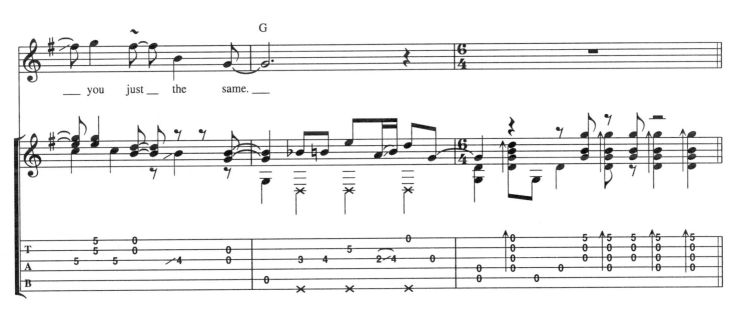

___ you just __ the same. ___

Worrying You Off My Mind

recorded by Big Bill Broonzy

Brownskin Shuffle

recorded by Big Bill Broonzy

Kokomo Blues

by Fred McDowell

Moderate shuffle
Introduction

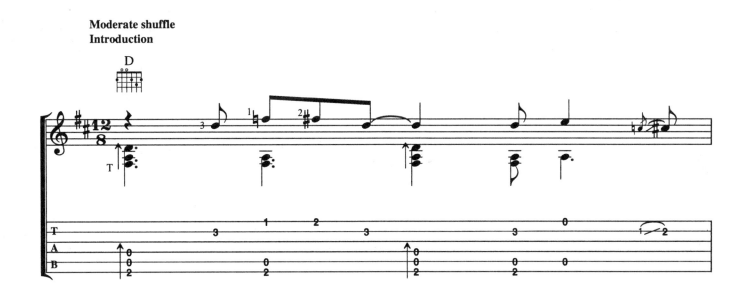

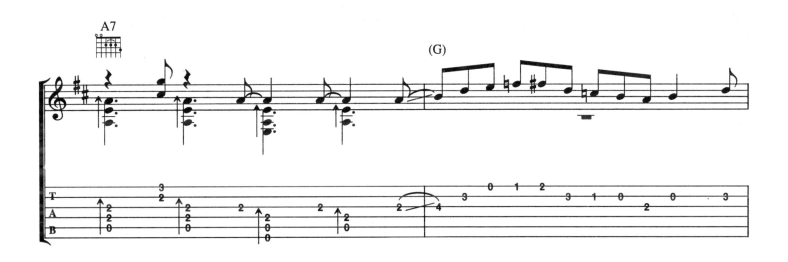

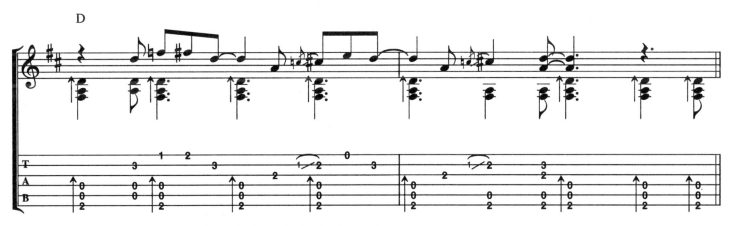

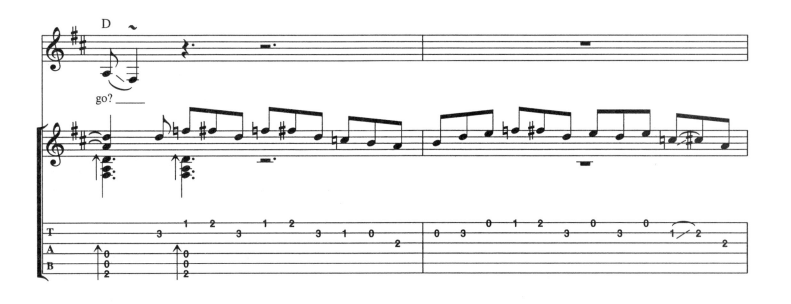

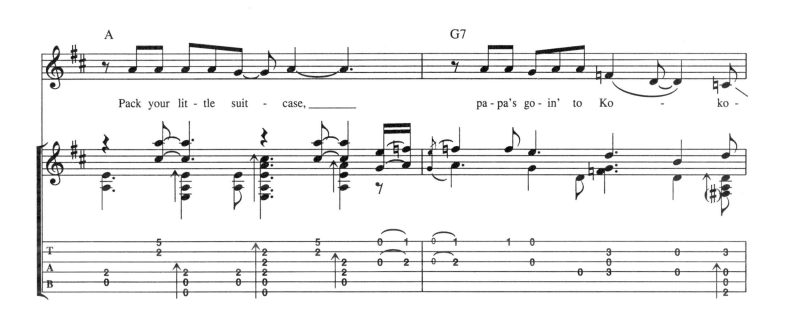

Pack your lit - tle suit - case, _____ pa - pa's go - in' to Ko - ko -

mo.

Alternate verse accompaniment

D7

D

G7

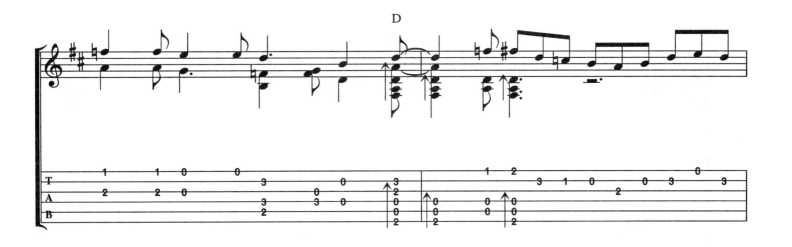

Away Down In The Alley Blues

recorded by Lonnie Johnson

Tuning: D G D G B E

Moderate shuffle

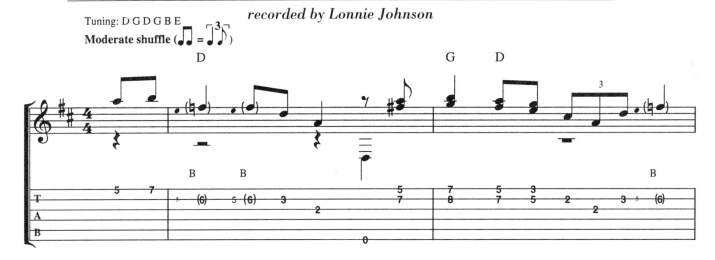

Verse 1

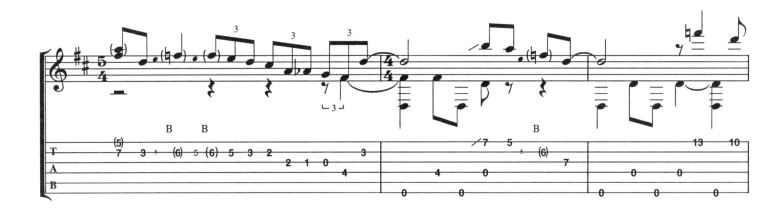

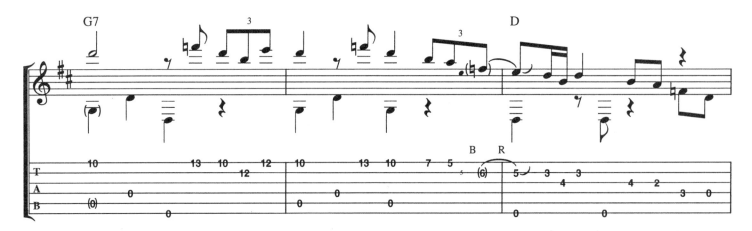

Verse 2

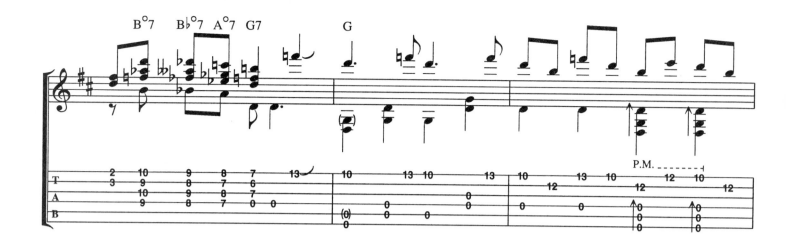

Verse 6

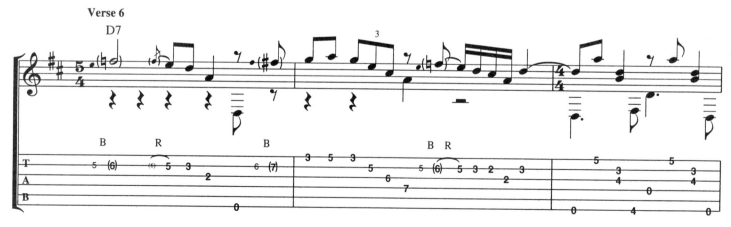

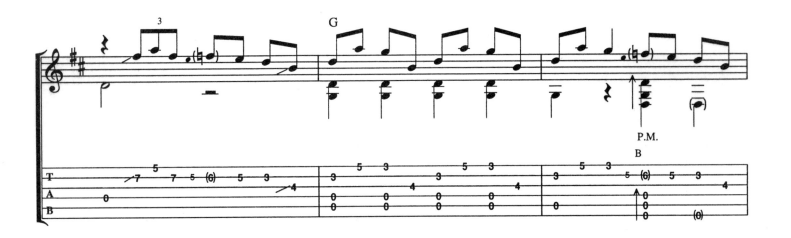

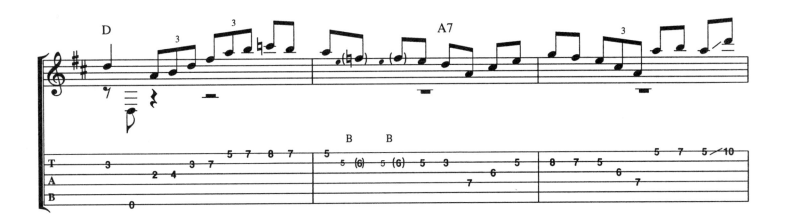

Statesboro Blues

by Willy McTell

Tuning: D A D G B E

Moderately
Introduction

Verse 1

1. Wake up, ma - ma, turn your lamp____ down low,_____

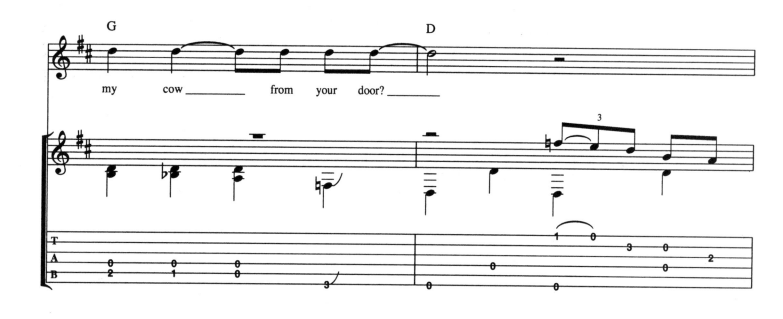

my cow _____ from your door? _____

2. My moth -

Verse 2

er died and left me reck - less, my dad - dy died and left me

wild,   wild,   wild, _____

G(7)

Moth - er _____ died _____ and left me reck - less,

Dad - dy died and left me wild, _____   wild,

D

wild,

No, I'm not _____ good - look - in', but _____ I'm some _

_____ sweet wom-an's an - gel child. _____

Traveling Riverside Blues

recorded by Robert Johnson

Tuning: D G D G B D
Moderately
Introduction

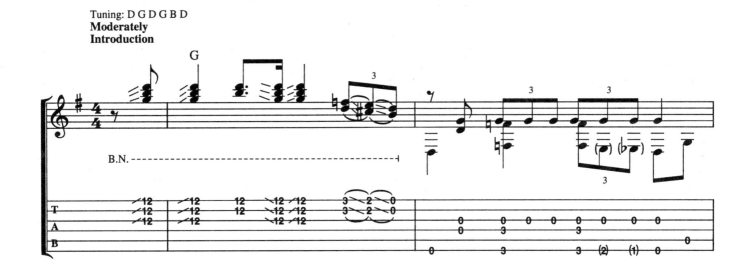

Verse 1

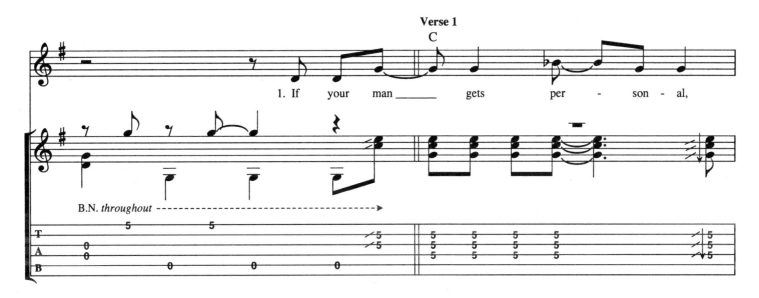

1. If your man _____ gets per - son - al,

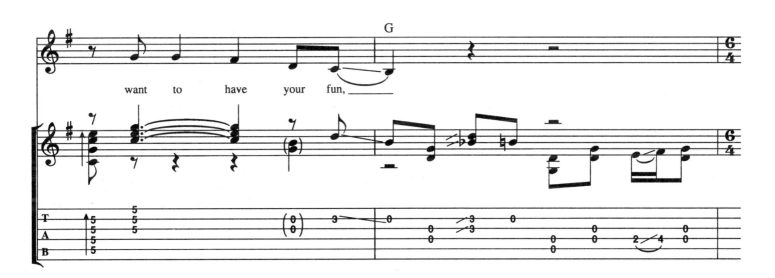

want to have your fun, _____

If your man _____ gets per - son - al, ___

want to have your fun, _____

Just come on back to Friars _ Point, ma - ma, and

bar - rel-house all night long. ___

57

But my Friars _____ Point rid - er now _ hops all o - ver me. _____

3. I ain't goin' to state no col - or, but her __ front teeth crowned with gold, _____

I ain't goin' to state no col-or, but her _ front teeth is crowned _ with gold, _

She got a

(D7)

mort- gage on _ my body now, _ a lien _ on my soul. _

(4. Lord I'm goin')

I Believe I'll Dust My Broom

recorded by Robert Johnson

Tuning: D A D G B E

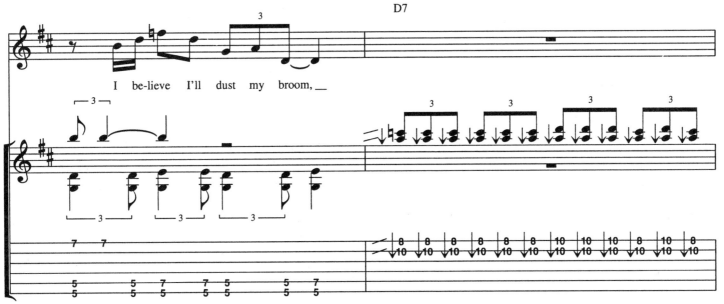

I be-lieve I'll dust my broom, __

Girl-friend, the black   man you been lov-in', __

girl-friend, can get my room. __

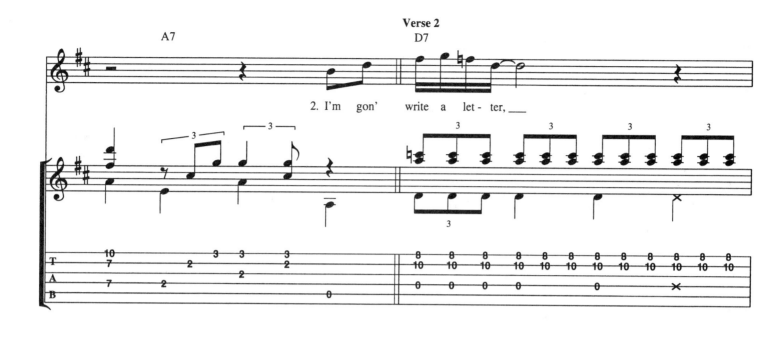

2. I'm gon' write a let - ter, ___

tel - e - phone ___ ev -'ry town I know, ___

I'm gon' write a let - ter, ___

Ain't No Tellin'

by Mississippi John Hurt

Moderately fast
Introduction

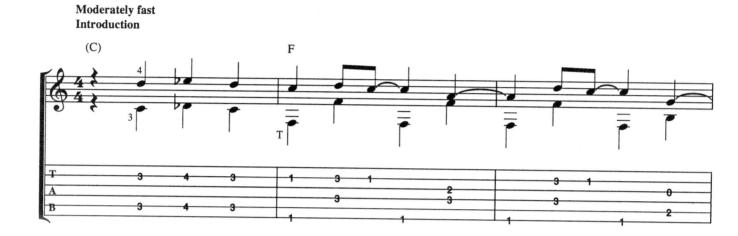

Verse 1

1. Don't you let _____ my good _____

_____ girl catch you here. _____ Don't you

Candy Man Blues

by Mississippi John Hurt

Moderately fast
Introduction

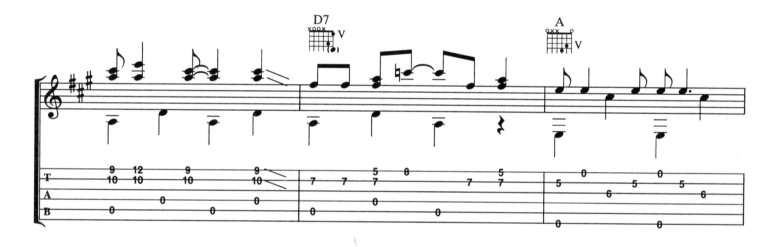

A

1. Now

Verse 1

A

all   you   lad - ies,   all   gath - er   'round,____   That

E7

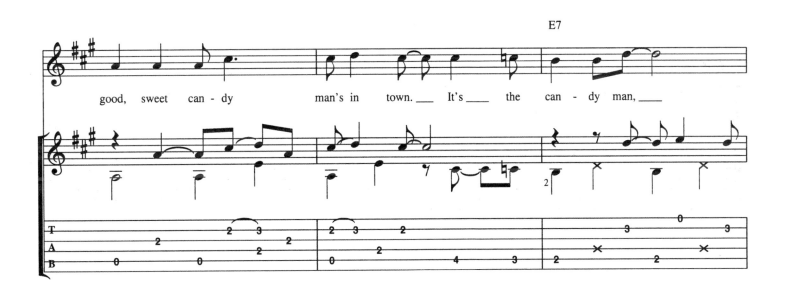

good,   sweet   can - dy   man's   in   town.____   It's____   the   can - dy   man,____

It's ____ the can - dy man.

Guitar break

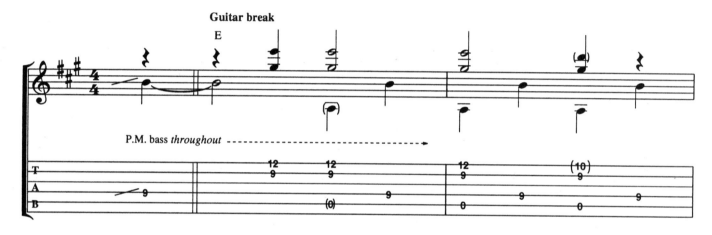

P.M. bass *throughout* - →

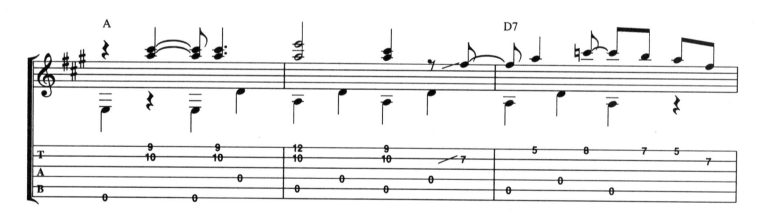

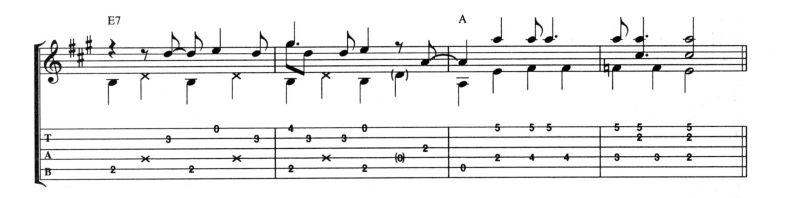

Alternate verse accompaniment

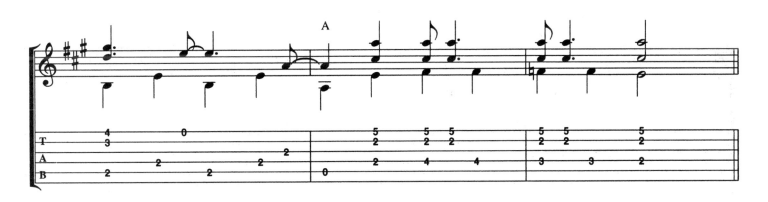

Green River Blues

recorded by Charlie Patton

Moderately
Introduction

Verse 1

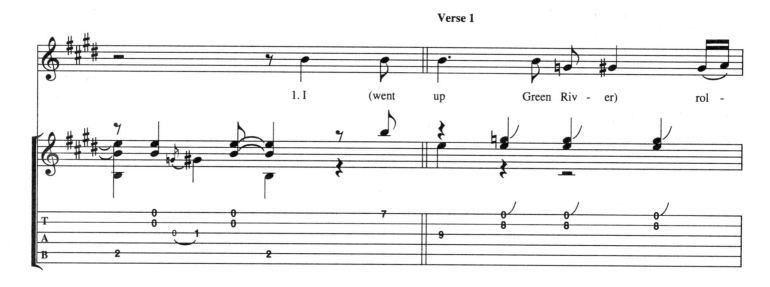

1. I (went up Green Riv - er) rol -

lin' _____ like a log, _____

wade up Green _____ Riv - er rol - lin' _____ like a _____

log, _____

I _____ wade _____

_____ up Green ___ Riv - er, ___ Lord, rol - lin' _____ like a log, ___

Alternate verse accompaniment (*first five measures*)

Screamin' And Hollerin' The Blues

recorded by Charlie Patton

Tuning: D G D G B D

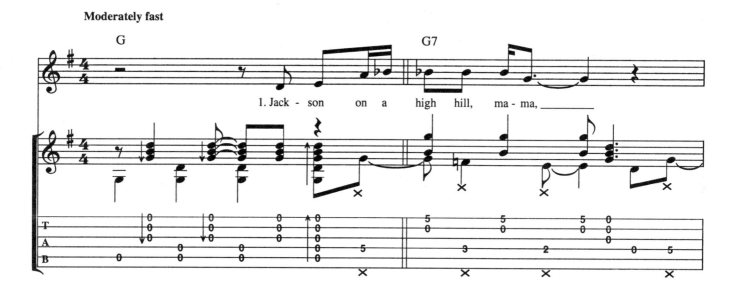

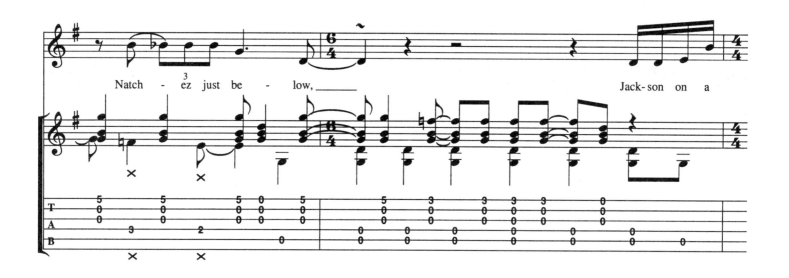

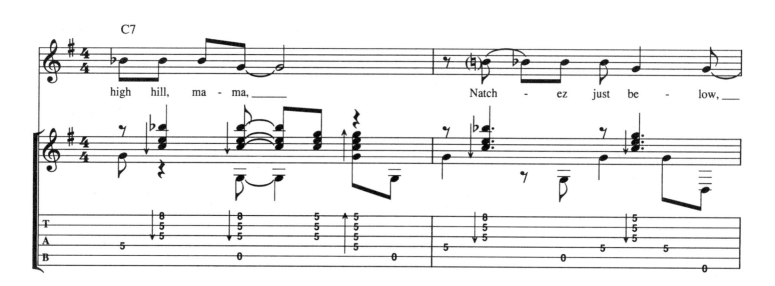

(Spoken: Certain days—you know how they are.)

I ev-er get back home, I ___

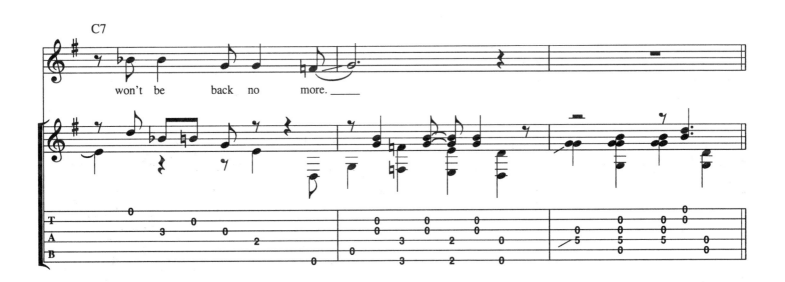

won't be back no more. ___

Alternate verse accompaniment (first four measures)

Alternate verse accompaniment (first four measures)

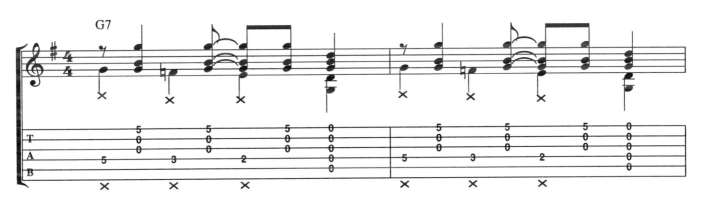

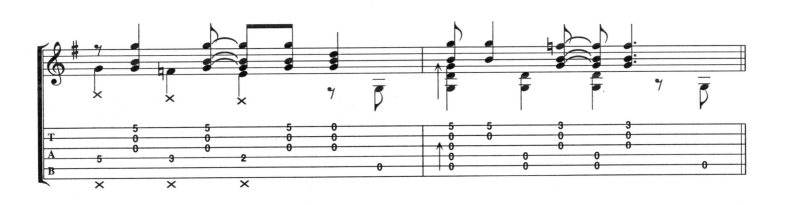

Mistreated Blues

recorded by Henry Townsend

Tuning: E B E G B E
Moderate shuffle
Introduction

1. My ____ ba-by just mis-treats me ____ night and ____ day,

If my sweet _

Bye-Bye Blues

recorded by Tommy Johnson

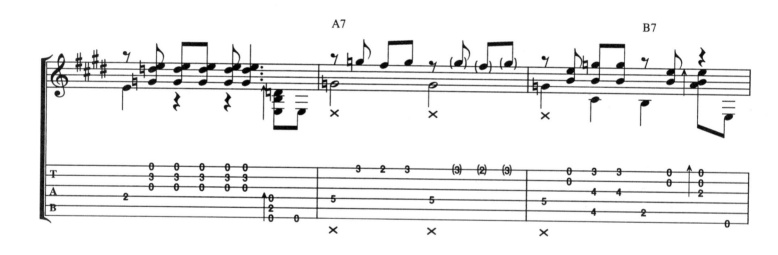

E

1. Cry - in' ____

Verse 1

____ bye - bye, ba - by, bye ____ and bye, ____

A

And bye and bye, ____ now ba - by won't you, bye and bye, ____

Alternate verse accompaniment

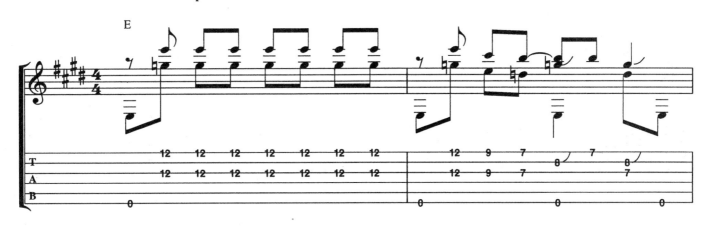

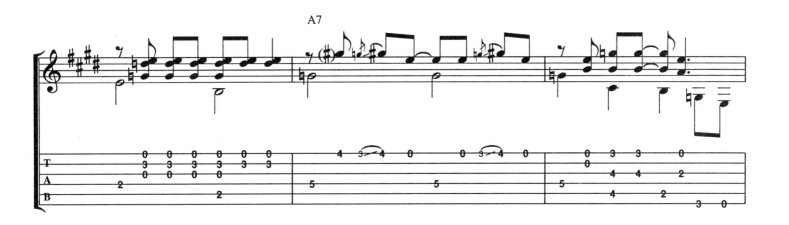

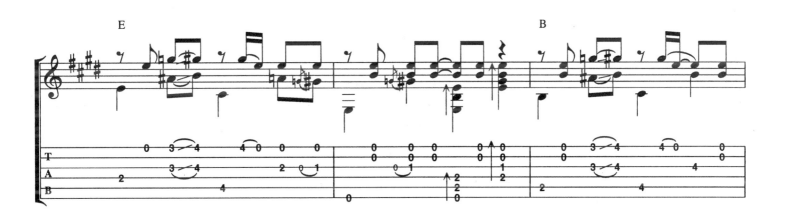

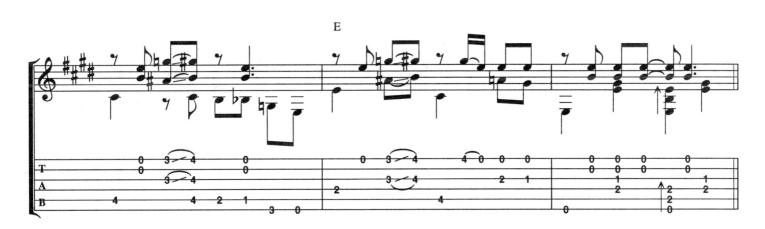

God Moves On The Water

recorded by Blind Willie Johnson

long?

How ____ long? ____

Verse 1

1. Year of nine - teen hun - dred and twelve, ____ A - pril the four - teenth

day, (Great) *Ti - tan - ic* (hit an) ice - berg, ____

Peo - ple there run and pray, God ____ moves, ____

moves, ____ God moves, ____

and the peo - ple there run and pray.

Guitar break
(D7)

B.N. *throughout* ------------->

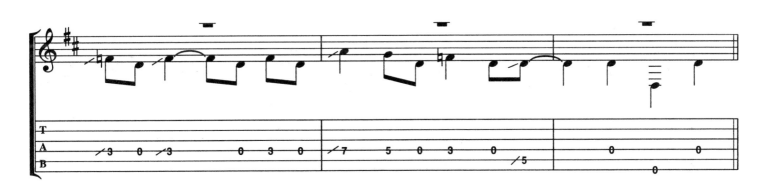

Georgia Bound

recorded by Blind Blake

First guitar break

Second guitar break

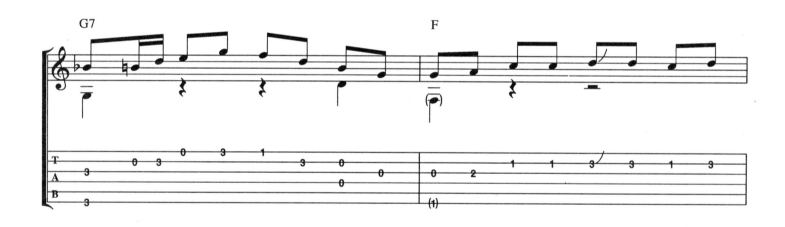

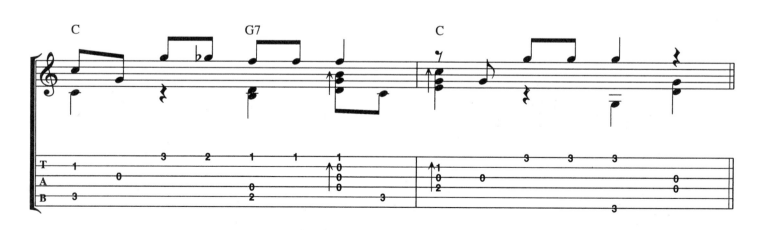

Police Dog Blues

recorded by Blind Blake

Tuning: D A D F# A D

Introduction

Moderately fast shuffle

Second guitar break

South Carolina Rag

recorded by Willie Walker

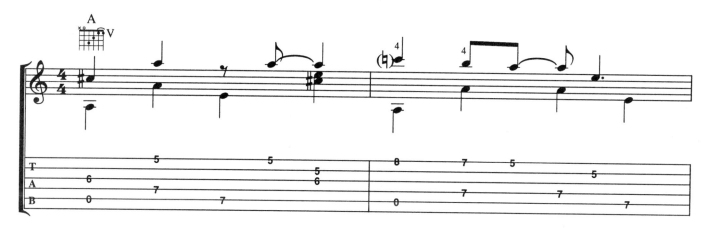

Hey, ___   *(spoken:* Play it, boy)   I want tell you,

that's no way to do.

Verse 1

1. Ask to drink wa - ter, (she) brought gas - o - line,

Now, let me tell ya, do - in' me migh - ty mean, ___

I ___ tell ya, that's no way to do. ___

Second guitar break

Hey,   hey.   (spoken: Play that thing, boy.)

Alternate verse accompaniment (measures 7 and 8)

County Farm Blues

recorded by Son House

Tuning: D G D G B D

Devil Got My Woman

by Nehemiah (Skip) James

Tuning: D A D F A D

Slow shuffle (♪♪ = ♪ ♪³)
Introduction

Drunken Barrel House Blues

recorded by Memphis Minnie

Moderate
Introduction

C.C. Rider

Words and Music by Huddie Ledbetter
Collected and Adapted by John A. Lomax and Alan Lomax

Tuning: D G D G B D

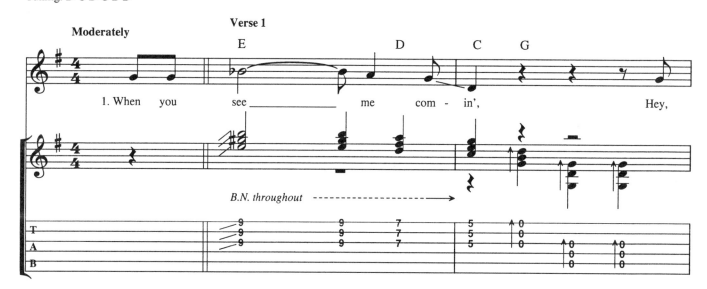

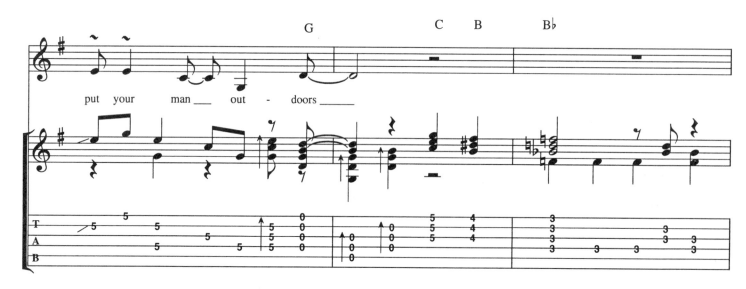

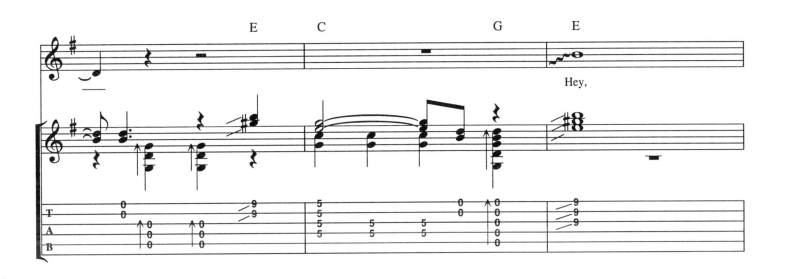

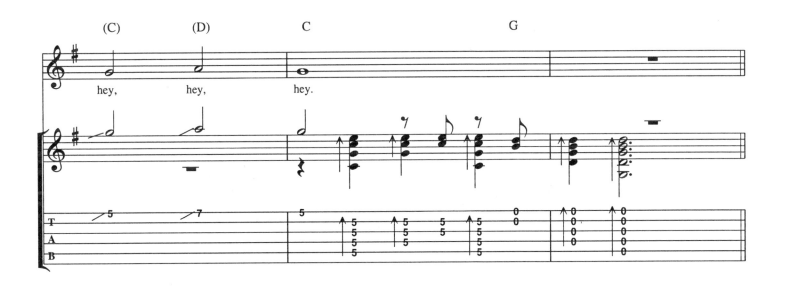

Who's Been Here?

recorded by Bo Carter

Tuning: D G D G B E
Moderately fast shuffle
Introduction

Verse 1

1. Ba - by, who's _____ been here _____ since your dad - dy been gone? Says _____ he must have been a preach - er, dad -

I Be's Troubled

Written by Muddy Waters

Tuning: D G D G B D

Moderately fast

Introduction

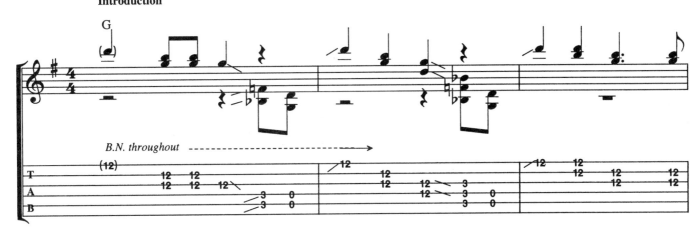

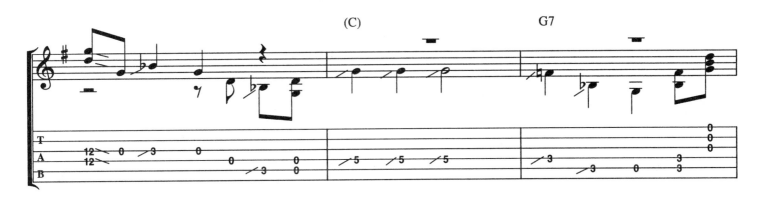

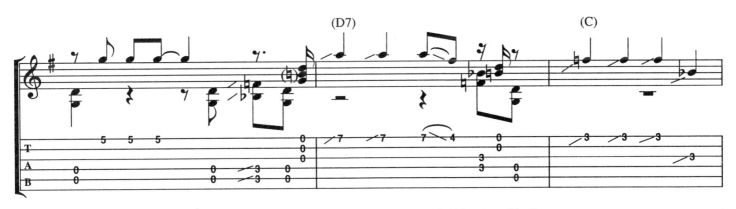

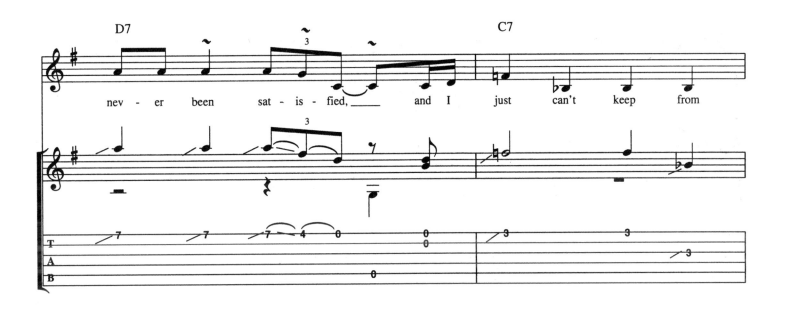

nev - er been sat - is - fied,____ and I just can't keep from

cry - in.

Meat Shakin' Woman

recorded by Blind Boy Fuller

men don't ___ look home. ___

Guitar break

* This measure may be omitted.

117

Weeping Willow

recorded by Blind Boy Fuller

and that mourn - in' dove, _____   I got a

gal up   the coun - try, Lord, _____ you know I sure do love. ____

I Am The Light Of This World

by Rev. Gary Davis

Chorus

Just as long as I'm in this world, _____

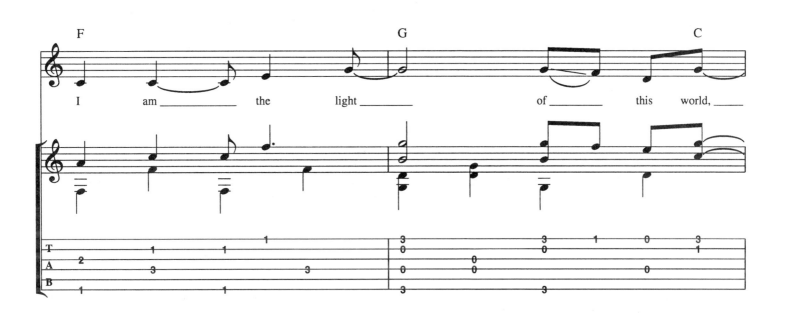

I am _____ the light _____ of _____ this world, _____

_____ Just as long as I'm - a in this _____ world, _____

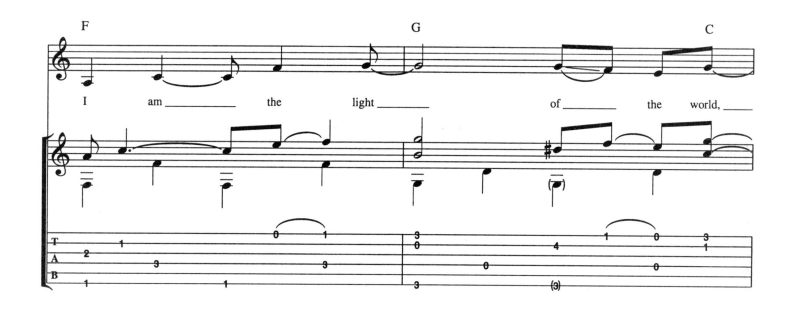

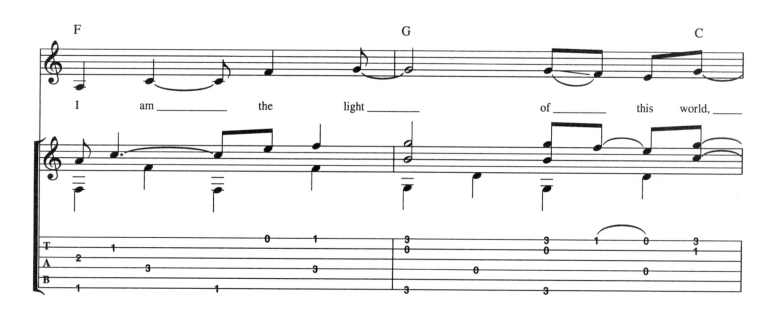

Just as long as I'm in _____ this world, _____

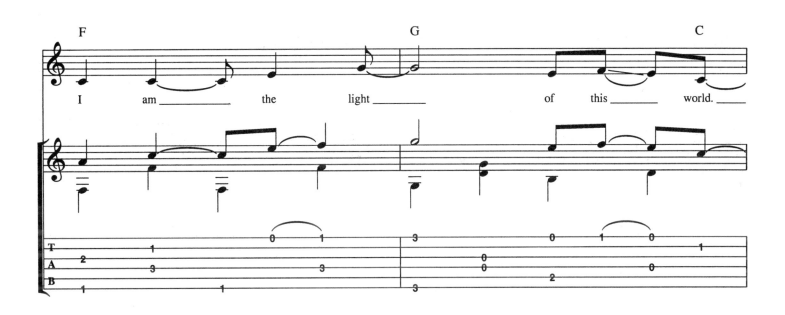

F   G   C

I   am _____ the   light _____ of this _____ world. _____

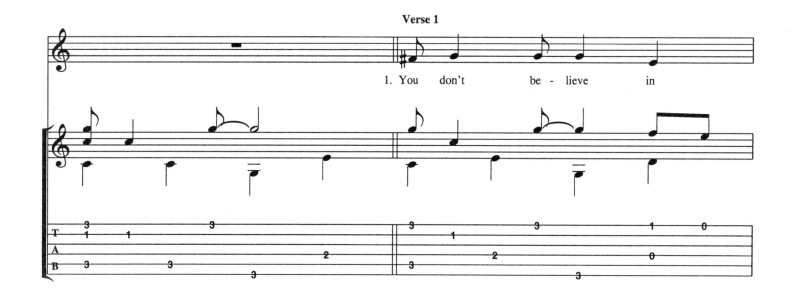

Verse 1

1. You don't be - lieve in

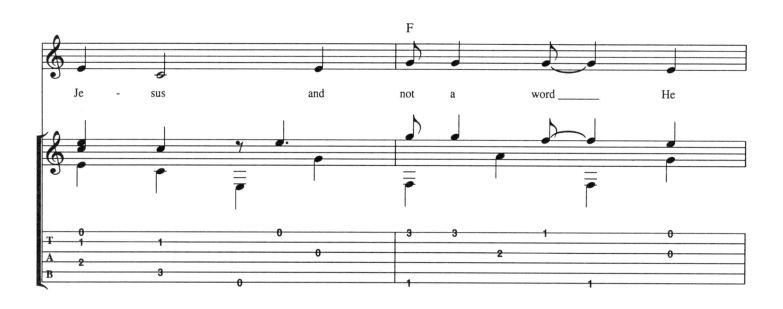

Je - sus and not a word _____ He

say, When He come all the way down to

Laz'- rus' grave _____ and raise him from the dead.

Alternate verse accompaniment (*measures 3 and 4*)

Make Believe Stunt

by Rev. Gary Davis

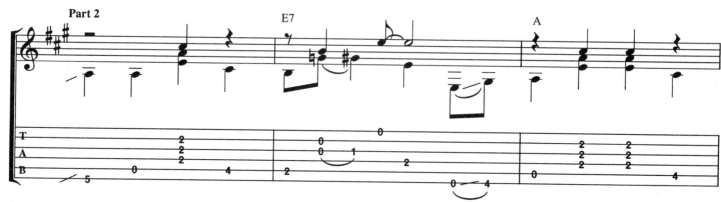

Dust My Broom

by Elmore James

Tuning: D A D F# A D
Moderate shuffle
Introduction

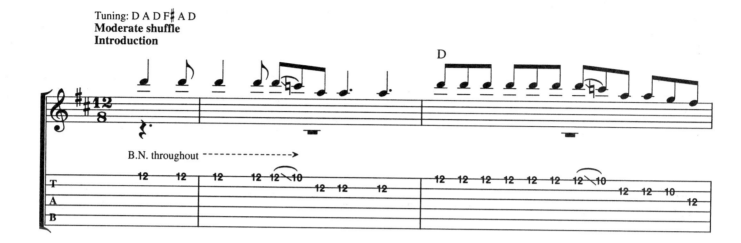

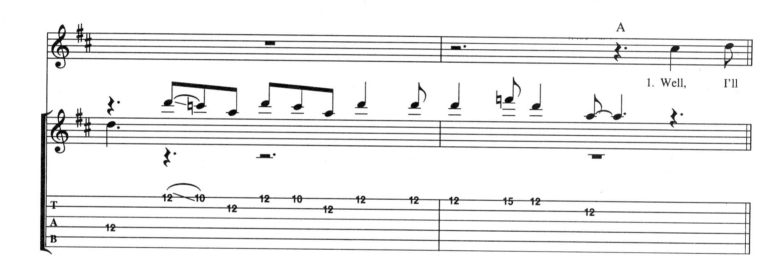

Verse 1

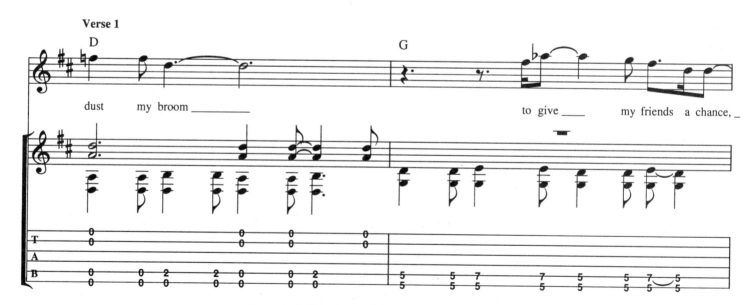

Ain't Goin' Down That Dirt Road

by Chester Burnett

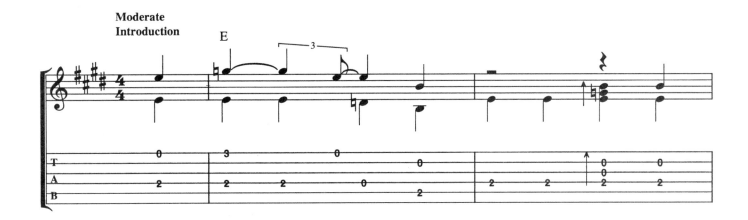

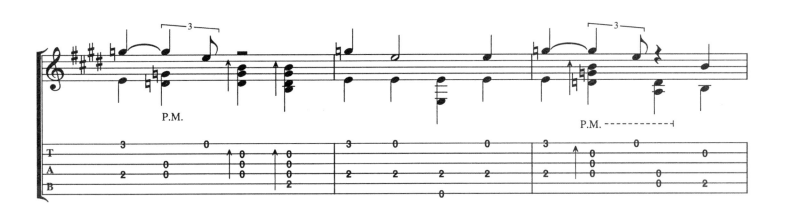

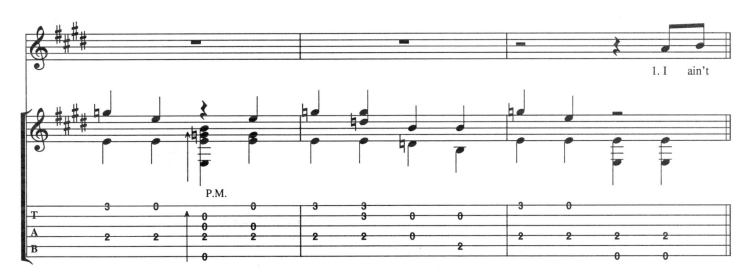

Verse 1

go - in' down _____

dirt _____ road _____ by my - self, _____

P.M. -------┤

134

Babe, I ain't go - in' down ____

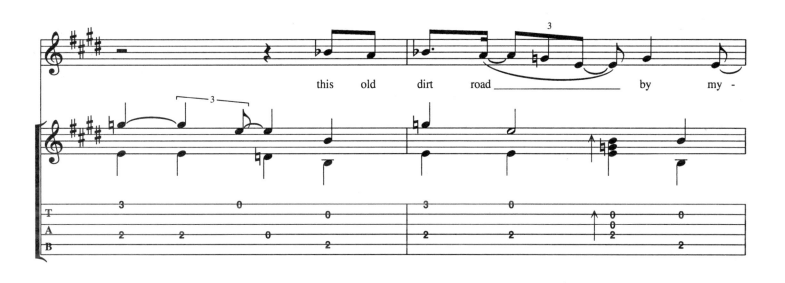

this old dirt road _____ by my -

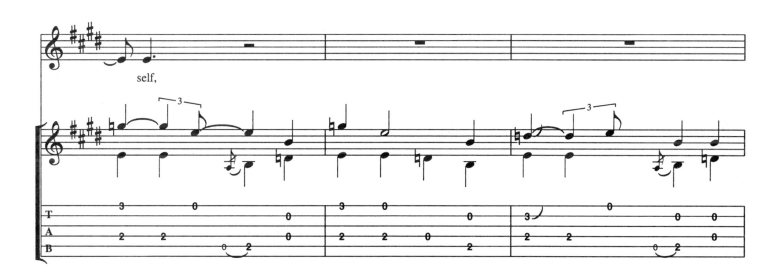

self,

If I

don't carry you, _____ ba - by, _____

I'm gon - na

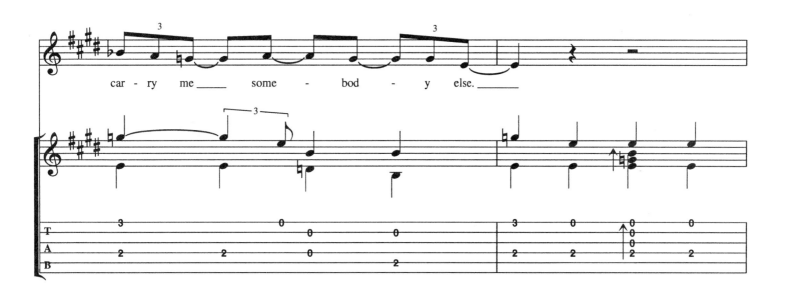

car - ry me ____ some - bod - y else. _____

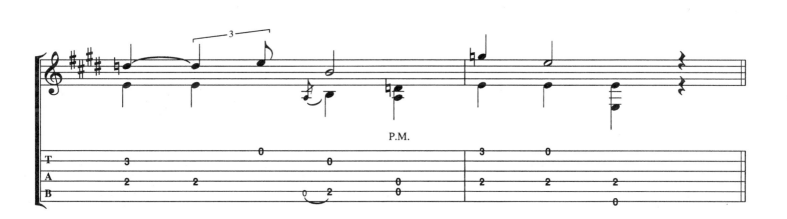

P.M.

Come Back Baby

recorded by Snooks Eaglin

Slowly
Introduction

1. Come back, ba - by, ___

Verse 1

___ Please ___ don't go, ___ For the way I love you, ba -

by,   You'll nev - er know. _____   Come back, ba -

by,   Let's talk it o - ver,   One more time. _

Sugar Babe

by Mance Lipscomb

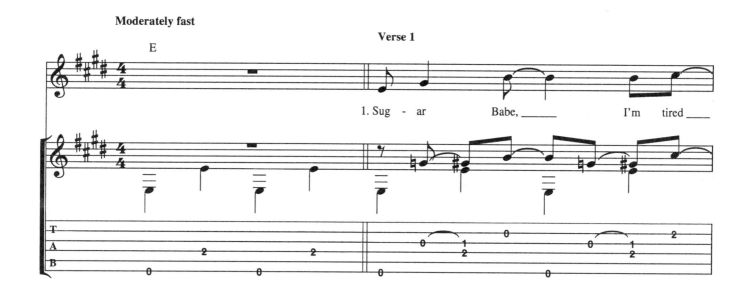

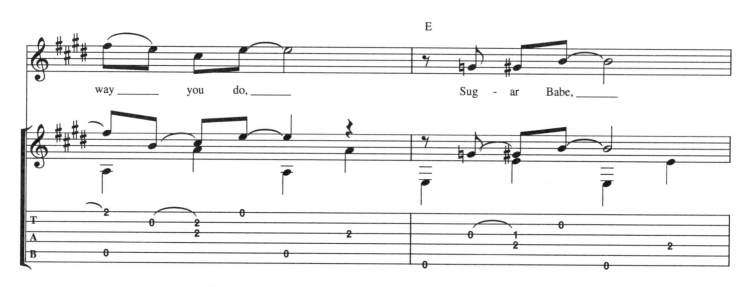

it's all ___ o - ver now. ___

Guitar break

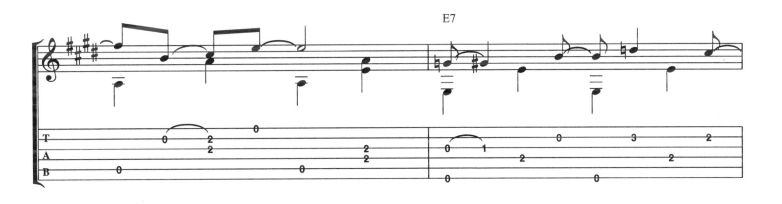

Baby What You Want Me To Do

by Jimmy Reed

You Got To Move

by Fred McDowell and Garry Harding Davis

Tuning: D A D F# A D

Slow heavy shuffle
Introduction

Verse 1

1. You got to move, you _____ got to move, You got to move, child, _____ you got to move, But when the Lord _____ get read - y, _____ you got to move. _____

145

Additional Lyrics

Ain't Goin' Down That Dirt Road

Well, darlin' you don't know the day have been,
A long, cold lonesome day.

You know the day have ( ) a long old lonesome day,
That's why I can't go down the dirt road by myself,
And if I don't carry you baby, I'm goin' carry me somebody else.

Baby, shake my hand, if you never see me no more, *(2x)*

Just tell me what I asked you baby, do you want to go with me? *(2x)*
I ain't goin' down dirt road by myself,
And if I don't carry you baby, I'm going to carry somebody else.

Fare you well, darlin', this here the end for me, *(2x)*
I ain't goin down, babe, this old dirt road by myself,
(See, I got to carry somebody.)
I ain't goin' down dirt road by myself.

by Chester Burnett
Copyright © 1993 Arc Music Corporation
All Rights Reserved. Used by Permission.

Ain't No Tellin'

I'm up the country where the cold sleet and snow, *(2x)*
Ain't no telling how much further I may go.

Eat my breakfast here, my dinner in Tennessee, *(2x)*
I told you I was coming, baby won't you look for me.

(Hey, hey—that's scooping the clam.)

The way I'm sleeping, my back and shoulders tired,
The way I'm sleeping, baby, my back and shoulders tired,
The way I'm sleeping, my back and shoulders tired,
Gonna turn over, try it on the side.

Don't you let my good girl catch you here,
She might shoot you, may cut you and stab you, too,
Ain't no tellin' what she might do.

by Mississippi John Hurt
Copyright © 1983 Wynwood Music Co., Inc.
All Rights Reserved. Used by Permission.

Baby What You Want Me to Do

Goin' up, goin' down
Goin' up down, down up, any way you want it,
Let it roll, yeah, yeah, yeah,
You got me doin' what you want me, baby, why you want to let it go?

Got me beeping, got me hiding,
Got me beep hide, hide beep, any way you want to,
Let it roll, yeah ,yeah, yeah,
You got me doin' what you want, baby, why you want to let it go?

by Jimmy Reed
Copyright © 1959 (Renewed) by Conrad Music, a division of Arc Music Corporation and Seeds of Reed
All Rights Reserved. Used by Permission.

Bye Bye Blues

Say the good book tell you, reap just what you sow,
The good book tell you, baby reap just what you sow,
Don't reap it now, baby, reap it bye and bye.

Said I'm goin away, wont be back till fall,
I'm goin away, Lord, baby wont be back till fall,
If I meet that gal, won't be back at all.

Well, there two trains running, running side by side,
There two trains running, baby, running side by side,
You got my woman, baby, I know you satisfied.

Candy Man

Well all you ladies gather 'round,
That good sweet candy man's in
town.
It's the candy man,
It's the candy man.

He likes a stick of candy just nine
inch long,
He sells as fast a hog can chew his
corn.
It's the candy man,
It's the candy man.

All heard what sister Johnson
said,
She always takes a candy stick to
bed.
It's the candy man,
It's the candy man.

Don't stand close to the candy
man,
He'll leave a big candy stick in
your hand.
It's the candy man,
It's the candy man.

He sold some candy to sister Bad,
The very next day she took all he
had.
It's the candy man,
It's the candy man.

If you try his candy, good friend
of mine,
You sure will want it for a long,
long time.
It's the candy man,
It's the candy man.

His stick candy don't melt away,
It just gets better, so the ladies
say.
It's the candy man,
It's the candy man.

by Mississippi John Hurt
Copyright © 1963 Wynwood Music Co.,
Inc.
All Rights Reserved Used by Permission

C.C. Rider

I tried to find country girl I know,
(3x)
Hey, hey, hey.

If I was a catfish, swimming in the
deep blue sea, *(3x)*
Hey, hey, hey.

Look a here, pretty mama, what
you got on your mind, *(3x)*
Hey, hey, hey.

Tryin' to fool, tryin' to fool the
man of mine,
Hey, hey, hey.

Words and Music by Huddie Ledbetter
Collected and Adapted by John A. Lomax
and Alan Lomax
TRO - © Copyright 1936 (Renewed)
Folkways Music Publishers, Inc., New
York, NY
International Copyright Secured.
Made in U.S.A.
All Rights Reserved Including Public
Performance For Profit.
Used by Permission.

Come Back Baby

For the way I love you, child, you
know I do,
For the way you love me, baby,
you never know,
Come back baby, lets talk it over,
one more time.

You know I love you, tell the
world I do,
For the way I love you baby, you
never know,
Come back baby, lets talk it over,
one more time.

County Farm Blues

Put you down on the man they call
Captain Jack,
Put you under (a) man called
Captain Jack, *(2x)*
You sure write his name up and
down your back.

Put you down in a ditch with a
great big spade, *(2x)*
Wish to God that you hadn't
never been made.

On a Sunday the boy will be
lookin' sad, *(2x)*
Just wondering about how much
time he had.

Devil Got My Woman

Oh, nothing but the devil changed
my baby's mind, *(2x)*

I laid down last night, *(3x)*
Tried to take my rest,
My mind got to rambling, like the
wild geese in the west.

The woman I love, *(3x)*
Stoled her from my best friend,
And he got lucky, stoled her back
again.

by Nehemiah (Skip) James
Copyright © 1965 Wynwood Music Co.,
Inc.
All Rights Reserved Used by Permission

Drunken Barrel House Blues

Catch me drunk in the morning,
don't say one mumbling word,
(2x)
I can't tell you all about it, and I
ain't gonna tell you nothin' I
heard.

Well I believe I'll get drunk, tear
this old barrelhouse down, *(2x)*
'Cause I ain't got no money, but I
can hobo it out of town.

Give me one more drink, drink of
that bottle and gourd, *(2x)*
And I will tell everybody just as
soon as I get back home.

Give me a stein of beer, if not a
drink of gin, *(2x)*
I feel myself getting sober, I want
to get back drunk again.

Dust My Broom

It's early in the morning, I believe
I'll go home, *(2x)*
I'm gonna quit my runnin' around
and never more to roam.

I went back home the next day, I
went home the next day about ten,
(2x)
But before that day was over, and
my baby started all over again.

I stay away from my baby, just as
long as I could, *(2x)*
I've got my suitcase all packed,
and this time I'm goin' for good.

by Elmore James
Copyright © 1951 (Renewed) by Arc
Music Corporation
All Rights Reserved Used by Permission

Georgia Bound

I got the Georgia blues for the
plow and hoe, *(2x)*
Walked out my shoes over this ice
and snow.

Tune up the fiddle, dust off the
bow, *(2x)*
Put on the griddle and open the
cabin door.

I though I was goin' to the north
land to stay, *(2x)*
South is on my mind, my blues
wont go away.

Potatoes in the ashes, possum on
the stove, *(2x)*
You can have the hash, but leave
it on the clove.

Chicken on the roof, babe,
watermelons on the vine, *(2x)*
I'll be glad to get back to that
Georgia gal of mine.

God Moves
on the Water

The guards who had been a-
watching,
(Stayed) but they were tired,
When they heard the great
excitement,
Then the gunshot was fired,
God moves, God moves, and the
people there run and prayed.

Captain Smith gave orders,
women and children first
Mannin' the lifeboats, (pilin' it
on, Lord, what a horrible crush),
God moves, God moves, and the
people there run and prayed.

(Men had to leave) a happy home
(all their paper assets),
Lord Jesus, will you hear us now,
help us in our distress,
God moves, God moves, God
moves, people there run and
prayed.

Women had to leave (their) lovin'
ones, (get them to safety),
When they heard there's another
one doomed, hearts they'd almost
break,
God moves, God moves, God
moves, and the people there run
and prayed.

E.J. Smith, mighty man, filled the
boat then he couldn't understand,
(Namin' the name, guardin' the
ten),
God moves, God moves, God
moves, and the people there run
and prayed.

Green River Blues

Think I heard the Marion whistle
blow,
I think I heard the Marion whistle
blow,
And it blew just like my baby
gettin' on board.

I'm goin' where the Southern
cross the Dog. *(3x)*

Some people say the Green River
blues ain't bad, *(2x)*
Then it' must not a been them
Green River blues I had.

It was late one night, everything
was still,
It was late one night, baby,
everything was still,
I could see my baby up on a
lonesome hill.

How long, evening train been
gone?
How long baby, that evening train
been gone?
Yes I'm worried now, but I won't
be worried long.

I'm goin' away, know it may get
lonesome here,
I'm goin' away, baby, you may get
lonesome here,
Yes I'm goin' away, babe, may get
lonesome here.

I Am the Light of This World

I've got fiery fingers, and I've got
fiery hands,
And when I get up in heaven,
going to join that fiery band,

Prayer is the key to heaven, and
faith unlocks the door,
That's why my God gave me the
key, and told me to carry everywhere I go.

I know I got religion, I know I
ain't ashamed,
For the Holy Ghost is my witness,
and the angels done signed my
name.

Didn't they take old John the
Baptist, and put him in a kettle of
oil?
My God got in there with him, and
they tell me the oil wouldn't boil.

by Rev. Gary Davis
Copyright © 1968 Chandos Music
(ASCAP)
Used by Permission

I Believe I'll Dust My Broom

I'm going to write a letter, tele-
phone every town I know, *(2x)*
If I can't find her in West Helena,
she must be in East Monroe, I
know.

I don't want no woman, wants
every downtown man she meet,
(2x)
She's a no good pony, they
shouldn't allow her on the street.

I believe, I believe I'll go back
home, *(2x)*
If you mistreat me here baby, but
you can't when I go home.

And I'm getting up in the morning, I believe I'll dust my broom,
I'm getting up in the morning, I
believe I'll dust my broom,
'Cause then the black man you
been loving, girlfriend, can get my
room.

I'm going to call up China, see is
my good girl over there, *(2x)*
If I can't find her on Philippine's
island, she must be in Ethiopia
somewhere.

I Be's Troubled

Yeah, I know my little old babe,
she gonna jump and shout,
That old train (   ) girl, and I
come walkin' out,
Lord, I'm troubled, and I'm all
worried now,
Yeah, I never been satisfied, and I
just can't keep from cryin'.

Yeah, I know somebody, some
been talkin' to you,
I don't need no tellin' girl, I can
watch the way you do,
Lord, I'm troubled, and I'm all
worried now
Yeah, I never been satisfied, and I
just can't keep from cryin'.

Yeah, now, goodbye babe, got no
more to say,
Just like I been tellin' you, girl,
you gonna have to leave my bed,
Lord, I'm troubled, and I'm all
worried now,
Yeah, I never been satisfied, and I
just can't keep from cryin'.

Meat Shakin' Woman

Says, I asked my woman, give me
her smallest change,
I said, hey, hey, give me her
smallest change,
And the dollars came dropping
down, baby, just like drops of
rain.

If you boys take my woman, you
can't keep her long,
I said, hey, hey, you can't keep
her long,
I got a new way of getting down
you monkey men can't catch on.

Said, for my dinner I want ham
and eggs,
Hey, hey, I want ham and eggs,
And for my supper, woman, I
wants to be with your legs.

Now, you let me feel your leg and
it feels so soft,
Hey, hey, and it feels so soft,
Said, you know what you prom-
ised me, baby, please don't put me
off.

Mistreated Blues

And it's baby, baby, what have I
done? What's wrong? *(2x)*
Ah, you mistreated me baby and
drove me 'way from my home.

But I'm goin' now, baby, and I
won't be back no more, *(2x)*
Ain't let you mistreat me, drove
me 'way from your door.

Mm, well, I might feel mistreated,
and I won't come to your house no
more,
Mm, baby, don't mistreat me,
'cause you know I'm young and
wild.

I said, baby, don't mistreat me
'cause I'm young and wild,
You must remember, baby, one
time you was a child.

But never mind never mind, babe,
I've got my eyes on you,
But it's never mind, I've got my
doggone eyes on you,
And some old day, pretty baby,
you'll do like I want you to.

Police Dog Blues

I shipped my trunk down to
Tennessee, *(2x)*
Hard to tell about a man like me.

I met a gal, couldn't get her off my
mind, *(2x)*
She passed me up, saying she
didn't like my kind.

I'm scared to bother around her
house at night, *(2x)*
Got a police dog, craving for a
fight.

His name is Ramblin', when he
gets the chance, *(2x)*
He leaves his mark on everybody's
pants.

Guess I'll travel, guess I'll let her
be, *(2x)*
Before she sics her police dog on
me.

Screamin' and Hollerin' the Blues

(Oh,) for my mama's gettin' old,
her head is turnin' gray,
My mother's gettin' old, head is
turnin' gray,
Don't you know it'll break her
heart, know, my livin' this-a-way?

I woke up in the mornin', jinx all
'round your bed,
If I woke up in the mornin', jinx
all 'round your bed,
(Children I know how it is, baby.)

Turned my face to the wall and I
didn't have a word to say,
No use a-hollering, no use a-
screaming and crying, *(2x)*
For you know you got a home,
mama, long as I got mine.

Hey, Lord, have mercy on my
wicked soul, *(2x)*
(Baby you know I ain't gonna
mistreat you.)
I wouldn't mistreat you baby, for
my weight in gold.

Oh, I'm goin' away baby, don't
you wanna go?
I'm goin' away sweet mama, don't
you wanna go?
(I know you wanna go, baby.)
Take god to tell when I'll be back
here anymore.

Shuckin' Sugar

Now if you don't love me, please
don't dog me around,
If you don't love me, please don't
dog me around, shuckin' sugar,
Like you dog me around, I know
you put me down.

I ain't know my baby, thinks she
wanted all of me,
I know my baby, thinks she
wanted all of me,
Every time she smiles, she shines
her light on me.

Oh, I said fair brown, something's
goin' on wrong,
I said, fair brown, it is
something's goin' on wrong,
This here woman I love, she (God)
been here and gone.

Oh listen, fair brown, don't you
want to go,
Oh listen, fair brown, don't you
want to go,
Won't you take this glass of water
where that brownskin man can't
go?

Lord, I'm worried here, worried
everywhere,
I am worried here, worried
everywhere,
Man, I get started here, and I not
be worried there.

South Carolina Rag (Take 2)

Talk about your girl, boy, you
ought to see mine,
Ain't so pretty, but she surely
dress fine,
That's no way to do.

Talk about your girl, ought to see
mine,
She's the sweetest gal in town,
I want to tell you, that's no way to
do.

Hey, hey, play that thing,
Hey, hey, play that thing,
I want to tell you, that's no way to
do.

Music man, ain't it grand?
Play that thing, boys, long as you
can,
I want to tell you, that's no way to
do.

Beg for water, bring gasoline,
Now let me tell you, ain't that
mean?
I want to tell you, that's no way to
do.

Talk about your brown, you ought
to see mine,
Ain't so pretty, but she's the
sweetest in town,
I want to tell you, that's no way to
do.

Hey, hey, mister music man,
I'll tell you that sure is grand,
I want to tell you, now, that's no
way to do.

When you beg for water, she bring
gasoline,
Then they tell me that ain't doing
me mean.

Hey, hey, play that thing,
Hey, hey,
I want to tell you, that's no way to
do.

Statesboro Blues

She's a mighty mean woman, do
me this way, *(2x)*
When I leave this time, pretty
mama, I'm goin' away to stay.

I once loved a woman better than
I've ever seen, *(2x)*
Treated me like I was a king and
she was a doggone queen.

Sister, tell you brother. Brother,
tell you auntie.
Auntie, tell your uncle. Uncle, tell
your cousin.
Cousin, tell your friend—goin' up
the country, baby, don't you want
to go?
May take me a fair brown, may
take me one or two more.

Big Eighty left Savannah, Lord,
and did not stop,
You ought to saw that colored
fireman when he got that boiler
hot.
Reach over in the corner, mama,
and hand me my travelin' shoes,
You know by that, I got them
Statesboro blues.

Sister got 'em, Daddy got 'em,
Brother got 'em, Mama got 'em,
Woke up this morning, we had
them Statesboro blues,
I looked over in the corner—
Grandma and Grandpa had 'em,
too.

Sugar Babe

All I want my babe to do,
Make five dollars and give me two,
Sugar Babe, it's all over now.

Sugar Babe, what's the matter
with you?
You don't treat me like you used
to do,
Sugar Babe, it's all over now.

Went downtown and bought me a
line,
Whipped my babe till she changed
her mind,
Sugar Babe, it's all over now.

Sugar Babe, I'm tired of you,
Ain't your honey, but the way you
do,
Sugar Babe, it's all over now.

Traveling Riverside Blues

Now you can squeeze my lemon till
the juice run down my—
(Till the juice run down my leg,
baby—you know what I'm talking
about.)

You can squeeze my lemon till the
juice run down my bed,
(That's what I'm talking about
now.)
But I'm going back to Friar's
Point if I be rocking to my head.

Weeping Willow

If you see my woman tell her I
should hurry home, *(2x)*
I ain't had no lovin' since my gal
been gone.

Where it ain't no love, ain't no
getting along, *(2x)*
My gal treat me so mean and
dirty, sometimes I don't know
right from wrong.

I lied down last night, tried to take
my rest, *(2x)*
My mind got to ramblin' just like
the wild geese in the west.

Gonna buy a bulldog, watch you
while I sleep, *(2x)*
Just to keep these men from
making the early morning creep.

You gonna want my love some old
lonesome day, *(2x)*
And it be too late, I'll be gone too
far away.

Who's Been Here

Baby, who's been here since your
daddy been gone?
Says he must have been a
jellybean, had long shoes on,
He had long shoes on,
He had long shoes on,
Says he must have been a
jellybean, had long shoes on.

Baby, preacher's in the pulpit,
just tryin' to save souls,
And his daughter's out on the
highway corner selling jellyroll,
Selling sweet jellyroll,
Selling sweet jellyroll,
Daughter's out on the highway
sellin' jellyroll.

The preacher's in the pulpit,
jumpin' up and down,
And the sisters in the amen
corner, they're saloon bound,
They're saloon bound,
They're saloon bound,
Then they're in the amen corner,
they're saloon bound.

You Got to Move

You may be high, you may be low,
You may be rich, child, you may
be poor,
But when the Lord gets ready, you
got to move.

You see that woman that walks the
street?
You see that policeman out on his
beat?
But when the Lord gets ready, you
got to move.

You got to move, you got to move,
You got to move, child, you got to
move,
But when the Lord gets ready, you
got to move.

by Fred McDowell and
Garry Harding Davis
Copyright © 1971 TRADITION MUSIC
CO. (BMI). Administered by Bug/
CHANDOS MUSIC
All Rights Reserved. Used by Permission.

Discography

Scrapper Blackwell	Kokomo Blues	*The Virtuoso Guitar of Scrapper Blackwell* (Yazoo 1019)
Blind Blake	Georgia Bound	*Ragtime Guitar's Foremost Fingerpicker* (Yazoo 1068)
	Police Dog Blues	
Big Bill Broonzy	Brownskin Shuffle	*The Young Bill Broonzy* (Yazoo 1011)
	Worrying You Off My Mind	*Do That Guitar Rag* (Yazoo 1035)
Bo Carter	Who's Been Here	*Bo Carter's Greatest Hits* (Yazoo 1014)
Rev. Gary Davis	I Am the Light of This World	*Pure Religion* (Prestige Folklore 14020)
	Make Believe Stunt	*Rev. Gary Davis* (Heritage HTCD 02)
		Gary Davis, 1935–39 (Yazoo 1023)
Snooks Eaglin	Come Back Baby	*Snooks Eaglin* (Folkways FA 2476)
Blind Boy Fuller	Weeping Willow	*Trucking My Blues Away* (Yazoo 1060)
	Meat Shakin' Woman	
Son House	County Farm Blues	*Delta Blues: Original Library of Congress Recordings* (Biograph BCD 118)
Mississippi John Hurt	Candy Man	*Mississippi John Hurt: 1928 Sessions* (Yazoo 1065)
	Ain't No Tellin'	
Elmore James	Dust My Broom	*Who's Muddy Shoes* (Chess CD 9114)
Skip James	Devil Got My Woman	*Skip James: The Complete 1931 Session* (Yazoo 1072)
Blind Lemon Jefferson	Shuckin' Sugar	*King of the Country Blues* (Yazoo 1069)
Lonnie Johnson	Away Down in the Alley Blues	*Eddie Lang and Lonnie Johnson, Vol. 1* (Swaggie SI221)
Robert Johnson	Traveling Riverside Blues	*Robert Johnson: The Complete Recordings* (Columbia C2K 46222)
	I Believe I'll Dust My Broom	
Tommy Johnson	Bye Bye Blues	*Jackson Blues 1928–1938* (Yazoo 1007)
Blind Willie Johnson	God Moves on the Water	*Praise God I'm Satisfied* (Yazoo 1058)
Leadbelly	C.C. Rider	*Library of Congress Recordings, Vol. 2* (Rounder CD 1045)
Mance Lipscomb	Sugar Babe	*Texas Songster* (Arhoolie CD 306)
Memphis Minnie	Drunken Barrel House Blues	*Memphis Jamboree* (Yazoo 1021)
Fred McDowell	You Got to Move	*Mississippi Delta Blues* (Arhoolie CD 304)
Blind Willie McTell	Statesboro Blues	*The Early Years, 1927–33* (Yazoo 1005)
Charlie Patton	Screamin' and Hollerin' the Blues	*Founder of the Delta Blues* (Yazoo 1020)
	Green River Blues	
Jimmy Reed	Baby What You Want Me to Do	*Jimmy Reed at Carnegie Hall* (Sweet Beat SBCD 3001)

Henry Townsend	Mistreated Blues	*St. Louis Blues* (Yazoo 1030)
Willie Walker	South Carolina Rag (Take 2)	*East Coast Blues* (Yazoo 1013)
Muddy Waters	I Be's Troubled	*Down on Stoveall's Plantation* (Testament T-2210)
Howlin' Wolf	Ain't Goin Down That Dirt Road	*Howlin' Wolf: The Chess Box* (Chess CHD3-9332)

Further Information

Many of the classic blues recordings have recently been made available by various record companies. The majority of the artists in this collection are spotlighted on CDs devoted entirely to their music. A good place to find these and other anthologies is Yazoo Records (P.O. Box 810, Newton, New Jersey 07860). Performance videos of Son House, Rev. Gary Davis, Mance Lipscomb, and others go right to the source and are also available through Yazoo. Instructional audio tapes and videos dealing with specific playing techniques and with the playing of individual artists such as Big Bill Broonzy, Blind Blake, Rev. Gary Davis, Lonnie Johnson, Robert Johnson, and John Hurt (among others) are available through Stefan Grossman's Guitar Workshop Company, P.O. Box 802, Sparta, New Jersey 07871. In England and Europe, the best source is Crossroads Music Co., Att: David and Susy Beswick, 439 Newchurch Road, Stacksteads Bacup, Lancs, England OL13 ONB.

For a factual look at the history of the blues through the music of Charlie Patton, I suggest Steven Calt's *King of the Delta Blues: The Life and Music of Charlie Patton* (New Jersey Rock Chapel Press, 1988).

About the Author

Woody Mann took his first musical schooling with Reverend Gary Davis, the legendary gospel, blues, and ragtime guitarist. He then went on to perform with John Fahey, Attila Zoller, Dori Previn, blues veterans Bukka White and Son House, and to record his own solo work. He continued his formal training at the Juilliard School and New York University while he studied jazz improvisation with noted pianist Lennie Tristano. Woody has recently performed at many international music festivals, recorded a new CD release, and completed a series of successful video and audio tapes focusing on the early masters of the guitar. He is currently performing solo concerts in the U.S. and Europe and is a faculty member of The New School for Social Research Guitar Center in New York City.